HOME GROUND

Living in the Country

Gladys Ogden Dimock

The Countryman Press, Woodstock, Vermont

© 1985 by Gladys Ogden Dimock

Library of Congress Cataloging in Publication Data

Dimock, Gladys Gouverneur Ogden.
  Home ground.

  1. Home economics, Rural. 2. Country life.
I. Title.
TX147.D56 1985   640'.9173'4   85-423
ISBN 0-88150-049-6
ISBN 0-88150-035-6 (pbk.)

Design by Leslie Fry

Printed in the United States of America

To the memory of Abbie Mae Whitney Chatfield, neighbor, teacher, and friend.

Contents

Introduction:
From There to Here

SOME TIME AGO, WHILE DRIVING ALONG THE MAIN STREET OF A village in Maryland, I saw the title of a sermon posted outside a church. "A rut," it said, "is a coffin open at both ends."

By contrast, adventure—a nongroove—is a matter of getting out of the rut to see what it is like on your own. It is a step-by-step process. You look ahead as far as you can realistically do, say about five steps, and then you concentrate on the immediate next step. You may not see very far ahead, but you do see what must be done next, and you have a general idea of what comes after. If what comes after is not exactly as you thought it would be—why, that is part of the adventure.

Not that it is always easy. Most people consider moving from one place to another a big bother, not to mention scary. And so it is, especially if you move too often, or if you have little or no choice as to your destination. It is an entirely different matter, however, if your move is not from *here* to *there*, but from *there* to *here*— an adventure in a change of life-style deliberately undertaken and enthusiastically pursued.

A life-style of your own amongst congenial surroundings, in which certain qualities of life are more important than the things you own or the amount of money (within limits) that you earn. And once you have set out to acquire it and have achieved its goals, all else becomes *there*: a wasteland of too many people, too much noise, boring routines, brittle friendships, and wasted hours that occupy whatever time you might have had for yourself.

In the American culture, *there* is most often a city or a suburb, since the majority of Americans live in that kind of environment. *There* involves a considerable financial investment: house, fittings, furniture, church, school, jobs. *There* is comfortable, even luxurious. But if you are living *there* and find it less than satisfactory, you have probably thought it over, talked about it, argued about it, and have almost decided that this life-style is not for you—not forever at least. You have probably wondered if a different life-style of your own devising would multiply your satisfactions and reduce frustrations. And your thoughts have probably included getting away from overpopulation, perhaps to a village, a small town, or even the country—a place where you can belong in a unique manner. In that case you are thinking of *here*, whether you realize it or not.

And you have good reason. No matter how skillfully you organize your life in city or suburb, it is always characterized by a splintering. Especially splintered is your time. It is split into short segments that must be fit together, seldom creating a useful or interesting pattern and usually under the stress of upcoming demands for your attention. Except at night, few of these segments occupy more than an hour or so, and often they occupy less than that. Too much time is spent in traveling between places, which are often at some distance from home and from each other. A commuter drives from home to the office or the station. A homemaker drives to the school, to the supermarket, to lunch with a friend, to a meeting at church. Often the time spent in driving totals more than that spent at various destinations. Furthermore, most of this time spent in transit is taken out of the best part of the day. In fact, it's downright frustrating. And if you are willing to change it—by moving from *there* to *here*—and if you have any feeling for the country, then one of the best options is to create your own home ground in a rural setting. Such a life is an integration of many activities, including a few specializations, into an interdependence that produces that special quality of life in the country.

How to fashion such a creative life-style and at the same time survive the adventure is the subject of this book. I neither propose, nor am I qualified to go into, technical details of country living in all of its many aspects. I am more interested in the general proposition of how one can get the most out of living in the country, such a life as my family and I have experienced for nearly forty-five years; how to avoid some of the pitfalls; and how to simplify, improve, or abandon some traditional or new-fangled ways of doing things. How to meet the challenges of country living (such as burst water pipes or a chimney fire) with a sense of triumph and satisfaction in learning something new. How to create a life full of flavor and activity and learning, rewarding even when the job has been an unpleasant one (like cleaning out a stable or a drain pipe). How to appreciate the amenities of country living (like driving to the supermarket on a hill road in full awareness of the countryside surrounding you, watching a little bird learn to fly, watching your child find some fascinating new occupant out in the woodshed, or waiting for the bread in the oven of a wood-burning stove turn to a golden brown, crispy and hot and good).

Looking back from the vantage point of some years, I have learned that one finds out who one is by discovering what one can do. I have also learned that country living provides more challenge to one's ability than life in any other environment can. Of course, one does encounter challenges in the city, and one learns to cope with them. But in the country it is more fun; there is a wider range and a greater need for ingenuity and experimentation. With a good country meal at the end of the day, an open fire in the living room, a comfortable bed at night, sweet dreams, and an early rising to get the cookstove fire built in order to start the new day with a hot cup of coffee and a proper breakfast. Then bring on the day. One thing you can be certain of is that today will be different from yesterday. And tomorrow will be different from today.

Another thing you can be certain of is that your values will be rearranged. The adventure of deliberately finding a place for the self that wants to create something of its own—a place and a life that satisfies and stimulates and is more rewarding than the routine of being entirely dependent on others—this will become as important to you as the traditional values and perceptions that you once accepted as a matter of course.

If you undertake the adventure of moving from *there* to *here*, the result will eventually be harmony. And harmony? After forty-five years, this is how my husband, Marshall, sees it:

> It is having a center to one's life. A place to live. Interesting work to do. Interests that are larger than one can hope to accomplish in a lifetime. A philosophy to use as a compass and to warm the spirit. Congenial people. Growth. Living close to nature. Exhilaration. Struggle. Enjoying the seasons. Trying to learn simple truths in primitive situations. Being oneself. (Marshall E. Dimock, *The Center of My World: An Autobiography* [Woodstock, Vermont: The Countryman Press, 1980])

Having lost my sight several years ago, I have had to change my writing habits. I have had to use a recorder, but especially I have needed the help of assistants who have unstintingly read manuscripts to me. Together we have revised and polished my overall view of a rural life-style.

The first of these assistants was Diane Brownell of White River Junction, Vermont, who became an able editor in her own right. The second was Mary Campbell Smith of Gaysville, Vermont. She fitted this work in with a wedding, a son, and a job. The third was Deborah Allen of Royalton, Vermont, a neighbor and also an author. She has contributed much time, editorial skill, ideas, a good sense of humor, and much pleasure to the author.

1

Where Is Here?

IF YOU WERE TO CHANGE THE PRESENT FLATNESS OF YOUR LIFE, the time-consuming routine, the mindless conformity of your values; if you were to seek renewal, revitalization, a new élan to your life; if you were to avoid the next inevitable "step up" which is sure to be expensive in terms of both money and peace of mind and instead create a more rewarding style; if you were to step into a way of life that renews your sense of adventure and learning who you are, where would you choose to live?

Surely at some point in your travels about the country during the past ten or fifteen years, on vacations or business trips, you visited or passed through an area that you remember with a special feeling. Perhaps you didn't realize its attraction at the time except in a visceral way, but the impression was made.

And it has stayed with you. The recollection of it comes back to you from time to time. Perhaps it has become part of your reveries. By now you can deliberately summon it into your consciousness.

It doesn't matter where that special place is. If you like it and feel comfortable there, if you feel in some satisfying way that you belong there, if something about it appeals to the inner you—a part of you that you have perhaps

1

ignored since your school days, or since that period of adjustment that follows commencement (and which is perhaps a real commencement)—then there is something in that particular area that has a nostalgic feeling for you. The vibes are right.

If there is a place like this in your background, then think about it. Maybe go and look at it again, to remember not only what it looks like but also what it feels like.

Or you can make a deliberate search at this point. Some people use a card system, listing places and their attributes. They weigh each factor and then compare localities by checking each locality for the same items. They narrow down the possibilities to a few, make a more intensive investigation, and then arrive at a final choice.

This is fine for some. People have different ways of making their decisions. But however you do it, it must be your way, whether unstructured or scientific, a combination of both, or something entirely different. If you do it your way, the results will be better for you. However, one basic rule is that *here* cannot be in a city or a suburb. If one of these is your choice, then you might as well stay where you are.

How you propose to earn a living after the move has been made should not be a determining factor at this stage. The main thing now is that the locality should suit you. This should be *it*. Although earning a living in a new environment is of importance, the details can be worked out in due course when you know better where *here* is. Finding compatible work in rural areas is seldom easy. Some ideas on the economic factors of living in the country appear in Chapter 15. These aspects of the matter make for yet another adventure.

Having found the right area, you now look for a home. Country condominium living is gaining popularity

today, especially in or near year-round recreational re-
sorts. While condos can be convenient and attractive—if
playing golf and skiing are the principal objectives for
moving—people who buy them are usually insulated from
the kind of *here* I am writing about. We preferred an older
home that could be restored—as much as possible by
ourselves. These are not easy to find, however, and have
become relatively expensive considering the amount of
money it will take to make such a house livable again.

Old houses are often remote. This should be taken
into consideration if you need the service of a school bus.
Although remoteness is often deliberately sought by city
people, it is impractical if you have a regular job or if
accessibility is something you regularly need. Still, I
recommend at least searching for an old house on an
accessible road. It is well worth it.

A perfectly satisfactory alternative to an old house is
building a house of your own, on land that you have
found suitable to your taste and need. There are two ways
to go about it: One way is to build a house that is as good
as an old place (well, nearly as good). The other way, which
is not just bad but which will defeat your very purpose in
seeking out the country, is to re-create the house you had
in the suburbs.

It is an easy trap to fall into. Your old washer may be
perfectly adequate, but a new one would look much better
in your new utility room. Your living room sofa is an old
friend, but it would look pretty shabby in your new living
room. Popular magazines offer a multitude of decorating
ideas designed to keep you in that rut—the open-ended
coffin of tradition—for all of the ideas require new things,
constructed of the most modern materials, and all of them
will prevent you from being able to find *here*. All of them
come from *there*, which you would leave behind.

So I leave it.

For there is an alternative. You can build a new *old* house. One that, like a truly old one, spreads a feeling of protectiveness, of welcome, and which reflects yourself as nothing else can. You can do it by starting with the smallest, most basic structure you can imagine living with. An unadorned box that contains the barest of necessities, with only enough space to squeeze everyone in. Put it up yourself, or hire a professional who will also wire it and install proper plumbing. It need only provide a place for the family to gather and for the family meals to be prepared. Sleeping arrangements of one sort or another, a bathroom, and a storage shed somewhere—that is all. Living with such a box will show you, and very soon, exactly what you need next. More privacy? Throw on an addition or finish off attic space for an extra bedroom or two. Storage for the wood supply? Add a woodshed. A porch for outdoor relaxation? Tack it on. Pretty soon your house will have character inside and out, character that no architect can design for you and that no builder can construct, because the house reflects the needs and per-sonality of you and your family. Within five years or so— presto—you have a new *old* house that will give you a sense of *here-ness*. You will be able to feel it, and it will grow the longer you live there. True, it takes a generation or so for new walls to acquire the special character of old ones; for the walls of a truly old house, one that has been lived in for several generations, seem as though they really could talk and are trying to talk to you. You can hear them, too, if you pay sympathetic attention. There has been happiness there, and tragedy, too. Births, deaths, quarrels, living, hating, irritation, joy, romance, hard times and good times, children scampering about, old folks still active and only occasionally retreating to the rocker by the fire. A lot of life has been lived within these old walls, and they reach out as though to say: We have known many good people in the past. Come and join them. We will keep you safe. Our experience is with such an old house, one abandoned and waiting for us to find it.

When you find a house that suits you—one that you want to work with and cherish and live in—you will know it as soon as you see it and even before you have set foot in it. There is that instant of recognition, such as sometimes happens between two people seeing each other for the first time. The house reaches out to you with an air of welcome and expectancy, like a lost dog that looks up at you and says, please love me, give me a home and someone to love. And you can't help but do it . . . and you can't help it with this house, either. You will cherish it from the moment you step over the doorsill.

No matter what the house is like inside, it is just right. No matter how run down or how much fallen plaster is lying around on the floors, no matter what the cellar or the roof looks like, if the foundation is firm and the house itself is steady and upright, all of these other things can be fixed. It will not be cheap, even if you can do some of the work yourself. But it will be yours, a part of you. You will know it, and the house will know it.

I have seen it happen this way on a number of occasions. For example, many years ago we took some friends on a search trip around our part of Vermont. After several inspections we followed an unlikely trail—it could not be called a road—to a brick house on a hill. The trail ended there, literally and figuratively. The house was empty and locked so we could only look through the windows. It was a rainy day, but we could see there was a view, cloudy and indistinct. The decision was made.

We sat on a covered porch and ate a picnic lunch, peanut butter sandwiches and cold coffee because the thermos had cracked and lost its vacuum. Back to the main road, we made inquiries, discovered the ownership of the house, and called on someone who knew about it. Then our friends had to leave. But they gave Marshall a blank check and asked him to buy the place for them. The following Sunday we caught up with the owner and gave him the check, five thousand dollars for the brick house, a barn, and a hundred acres of land with a brook running through it. Thirty years later our friends are still living there. Over the door in large letters they have written, "Heaven Can Wait."

Our own experience, only ten years earlier, was similar. Both Marshall and I were drawn to the central part of Vermont. All of Vermont is attractive, but north of the White River is a simpler, predominantly farming type of country. So we chose that region and set out to find the house. On a cold, wet day at the end of May we stopped for lunch at a small hotel in Bethel. As was our procedure, we asked around. Did anyone know of a place for sale? Someone referred us to the town clerk. We called on him. He said, yes, he did know of several places. He liked brick houses, he said. Did we? We hadn't thought about it but yes, we did. He gave us a map with four places marked on it with the comment that the gift of such a map had always resulted in a satisfied taxpayer.

With map in hand, we set out. It was early afternoon, and the rain was still coming down. We passed the first two places without stopping. Then we headed up a small valley along a brook to a crossroads, noted an abandoned one room schoolhouse on our right, turned left. We drove up a steep incline along the side of a ridge. The road was bad with a deep gully in the middle, in places almost too wide for the car to straddle. At the top we came into a clearing with a few great maples lining the road. A huge weathered barn lay ahead on the left, a small cottage also on the left. And on the right was a small brick house with an ugly dormer above the front door. The house looked at us for a

6

moment, as we looked at it. Then it reached out and embraced us, as we embraced each other. We got out to see what we knew would be ours.

The house was empty behind a front door that was merely closed, not locked. We stepped in. Stairs went up at the right. Flanking the hall were two front rooms. At the rear of one of them was a small area, traditionally called a birthing room, where a woman would go for labor and the birth of her child. Beyond the hall was a big dining room, beyond that a big kitchen and pantry, then a summer kitchen, and woodsheds, one of which contained the privy. Plaster was cracked and falling. No electricity. No sign of water except in the cellar, which was afloat. No fireplaces, but a chimney at each end of the main part of the house.

Upstairs there were three bedrooms in front, one of them in the big, ugly dormer over the front door. We would have to change that. Four more rooms stretched out toward the back, over the kitchen and sheds. Pretty shaky out that way, too. Later we learned that a man weighing more than three hundred pounds had rented the last two bedrooms for himself and his "housekeeper." Then they had moved in together and sublet the spare room. But the shakiness was not all due to him. There was also the matter of rotting sills below.

Back in the car, we returned to Bethel, discovered the owners of the property, and made them an offer. The following day we closed the deal for seventeen hundred and fifty dollars, paying five hundred dollars down and mortgaging the remainder. We now owned a house, a huge barn, a small cottage, and one hundred and thirty-five acres of forest, pasture, and meadow, with a brook running through the property.

It took several years to restore the house. World War II was still in course and we had little time away from Washington. A professional builder did the major part of the restoration at a dollar per hour for the contractor when he was on the job, seventy-five cents per hour for the master carpenter, and fifty cents per hour for his helpers. Later, we did most of the interior work ourselves.

The fact that everything had to be done slowly, over two or three years, was a major advantage. Most people have an incurable urge to do everything at once, right now, forthwith. That is how we make mistakes. It is better to live in a house and meet its needs as they occur, or as you perceive them. This is especially true in an old house, which gives up its secrets slowly as it gains confidence in your judgment. Moreover, the work is never complete. When restoration is done, or done for the time being, there is the matter of maintenance. A little each year is an ongoing responsibility.

When the first stage of our restoration was complete, we still lacked electricity, partly because none was available and partly because we were content with oil lamps. We also lacked plumbing, except for a toilet, because the only water supply was from a spring under gravity feed, which supplied a small pipe to the kitchen sink and another to what would serve as a bathroom. But it did have many things no contractor could supply. A comfort, a coziness, a warmth that went beyond the wood-burning kitchen stove and the fireplaces we had installed. It had something to do with the spirit.

As time went on—and by time I mean thirty or forty years—we made additions to the house, including one big woodshed to replace the old ones, an addition to the kitchen, making it really big with dining and sitting areas hitched to it, and a detached study up over the retaining wall in back of the shed. When it became available, we installed electricity. And later a bathroom. We also developed lawns and planted gardens, fruit trees, and shrubs. We built a series of three ponds in the brook. And everything we did appeared to please the house, which seemed to stroke us as one might stroke a kitten.

Equally important, however, is the fact that nothing we did to the house to make it more convenient, and nothing we did to the grounds to make them more attractive, changed the simple life-style with which we started, and now, after more than forty years, continue.

Vermont as a place to live has changed a great deal since World War II, and almost everything is more expensive than it was when we arrived. The reason is a mystique that the state has acquired. It remains an enclave, separated to some extent from the horrors of the crowded culture of the nation. Although many of its old traditional values have been altered by the leveling influence of television, many are retained. The attraction remains; the interstate highway system has brought many so-called flatlanders to our hills despite soaring real estate prices.

When we came to Vermont, a person could not call himself a Vermonter unless his grandfather, and possibly his great grandfather had been born there. There is the story of a young stranger visiting a Vermont village. He stopped to comment on the weather to a man working in his yard. There was no reply. The stranger noted the bright sunshine. Still the man was silent. Then the stranger said, "My grandfather lived in that house over there." "Oh," said the man in the yard, "Guess it might be a nice day at that."

With the influences of the outside world creeping in, however, that span of time has been shortened. After only forty years, we are now called, or at least assumed to be, Vermonters. It is with a sense of humility that we recognize this. We are honored. The effect was achieved without conscious effort, it came along with our work and our life-style. And now that it is done, somehow we feel that we have entered the promised land.

Nevertheless, Vermont is not the only place in the United States where one can develop a life of one's own. Northern New York State, for example, has a host of lovely villages and small towns set among hills and lakes. Northern Michigan and the rest of that northern tier of states I'm sure have many lovely spots and interesting communities. In the Rockies are many secluded places. I recall coming down on the south side of Wolf Creek Pass in Colorado to a land of plains, hills, and small settlements. Farther south, the Sun Belt must be pretty crowded by now, but in the prairies and along the Mississippi River surely there are small enclaves of quiet and beauty. West Virginia still has lovely areas that are not too crowded. No state is without its attractions and possibilities for new adventure, the adventure of making a new start, using all that one has learned in the past, and putting it to use in a new place that liberates the spirit.

2

Restoring an
Old House

So, you have chosen to buy an old house instead of building a new one. Your friends think you are crazy. And if you did not have a good imagination, the ability to see that old house as it could be instead of the dilapidated old thing that it is, you would think so, too. You would have been turned off at the outset. Fortunately for you, no matter how discouraging the place looks at first, you have made the right decision.

The right decision, that is, if now you will avoid the worst mistake you can make: the determination that everything you want to do to this house must be done at once, the day before yesterday if possible. This is the single worst mistake you can make, that which will undermine your objectives.

Building a new house can proceed as quickly as your plans, your contractor, and your financing will permit. It is largely a matter of technology, having all the materials to build according to a blueprint that you have approved.

But with an old house, not so fast. It is a more subtle matter. For one thing, you have to ask permission of the house to do the things you propose. The position and condition of certain beams and stringers and partitions will partly determine the answer. There may be no room for a closet in the master bedroom; it may have to go in the bathroom, thereby reducing the size of the bathroom. Where, then, should you put the john? And so on. An old house also has a number of built-in problems, such as an improvised water system or electrical system. If there is no bathroom at all, finding space for one may call for a good deal of ingenuity. Ceilings are generally low, but may be high, which makes for extra heating. Windows may be in the wrong place, foundations inadequate, sills rotting, and the roof at the borderline between repair and renewal. You wonder where to begin. Everything clamors for immediate attention, and the tension, impatience, and frustration build up in you.

The best thing would be to camp out in your house for a season to become familiar with its needs, and then draw up a list of priorities. And do as much of the work as possible yourself. This will strengthen the alliance you have formed with the house. You may even start talking to it—and better still—listening to its answers.

Fortunately, when the workmen you hire come on the job, their progress will be slow. This is a tremendous asset, though you will chafe at delays. For example, if the carpenters knock off for two weeks in hunting season or to complete a job started earlier for someone else, you will have time to reconnoiter, to judge what has been done, to make changes in your plans. Perhaps the house will not be finished by the time you must go back to the city for the winter. This also can be an asset, for you will have more time to think about it and find a better solution for some of its problems, such as where to put the porch and how large to make the shed. Be glad you can take time over things like this. The house will be the happier for it—and so will you.

In our case the restoration was helped rather than

hindered by the fact that through our own carelessness much of it burned down: all but the brick part, and even that was damaged. Of course at the time we did not see the fire as an asset, because it was a horrendous experience, happening one Sunday afternoon only a month after we had taken possession. But we got a hint of the favorable side the following day when a neighbor looked in through a burned out window, shook his head, and remarked that we had "burnt up an awful lot of dirt"; the accumulation of years, falling plaster, and an attic full of debris. Fortunately the brick part of the house remained fairly intact and, starting from there, we rebuilt and restored, ending up with a somewhat smaller house and one easier to live in and care for.

We lived in the cottage while the restoration was in progress. The work was finished on Marshall's birthday at the end of October. We moved in, cooked our first meal in the brand new kitchen (new because the lumber was new), and that night slept in the master bedroom whose walls were still smudged with smoke marks and char. We left the following morning for Washington, not to return until the next summer, some eight months later.

For the house it was a profitable winter, because we spent most of our leisure time making plans, changing and switching the plans, returning to the original ideas, and then changing them once again. By the time we took up interior restoration, we knew pretty much how we wanted it.

In the years that followed we have made further changes, including the addition of a large woodshed, a separate study, an enlarged kitchen, a half bath upstairs— and electricity. But we never did install a furnace, and still lack such a thing. We don't need it, despite winters that sometimes touch the thirty degrees below zero mark.

When restoring an old house the place to start is with

the foundations. If these need attention, now is the time, because any work done on them in the future will disturb the whole house. Presumably, the foundations are in pretty good shape or you would have thought twice before buying the place. Ours are of large stones solidly fitted together without mortar, topped by granite slabs. The brick walls are set on these. In a frame house the stone foundations are topped with large beams called sills, and the frame of the house is attached to these. Wooden sills and beams wear out or rot, depending on conditions, and must sometimes be replaced or reinforced. All sills, beams, and joists ought to be tested for internal rot. The method is to drive a knife blade into them. If they are damaged, the blade will penetrate as much as an inch or two. In our case, after more than a hundred years our sills and beams were, for the most part, good.

In an old house the cellar floor is usually of dirt. In our case it is dirt and always damp, for it is close to the water table. In addition, during the spring it seems to stand in the path of one of the freshets on our hillsides. But no matter. We installed our water pump on a concrete platform. If there is a time when we can't get to the cellar without rubber boots, such a season is relatively short. We could install a sump pump, and I understand the next generation plans to do this. But for us it is not necessary. Some people go to the expense of installing a concrete floor, but to us the only real inconvenience of a wet cellar is that it is no good for storing root vegetables, and we have found other means of doing that.

Above the cellar, floors may need mending or replacing, or merely covering with a second layer of boards. This I recommend for added strength and for a measure of insulation from a damp cellar. The second flooring should, of course, be laid crossways to the original boards.

How your floors are refinished depends on you. A guide to any restoration is the degree to which one is a perfectionist, or is merely fussy. Neither is very useful. But there is no harm in indulging in these propensities if the finances will stand them. In fact, in the matter of floors, ours are rough but carpeted, except in the kitchen and bathroom where traffic is extra heavy. Linoleum is a no-no, especially in the kitchen, which in a country home gets a tremendous amount of wear and tear. For example, I can always tell what season it is by what I sweep up off the kitchen floor. In winter it is ice and snow tracked in from the shed which, when melted, makes for little pools of water. In spring it is mud, in the summer it is grass clippings, and in the fall it is dry leaves. Then at all seasons there is what comes in from the barn, and I once counted five different kinds of manure in one day, from cow to chicken to pig and pony, plus dog. The last an accident, but the others carelessness. One also tends to drop heavy things, like a stove lid. Escaped sparks or embers from the fire box also add their trademarks. So I have counted it lucky that I have never had lineoleum on my kitchen floor.

All floors can, of course, be top dressed with waxes, synthetic washes, and the like. Fine for those who need them. And fine until they must be removed.

As for walls, these can be plastered and painted, papered, or paneled. Ours are either plastered and painted, or paneled. Wallpapering is traditionally done by the women in this part of the country. A woman will assemble her materials and her female neighbors, and they will spend the day at a job, with lunch provided by the hostess. In former days the ceilings also were papered. But paper becomes dingy and tattered, and we have never had it. Where we have paneling, it is weathered gray barn boards, yellow birch, or pine. In some cases the ceilings are painted. In others we used plywood, but that was a mistake, if only for aesthetic reasons.

In restoring an old house the greatest challenge is rearranging rooms, in the first place to accommodate a bathroom and closets. This may take a good deal of ingenuity. Sometimes you put up with the possible. In our own case the bathroom is in effect a passageway between the kitchen and the master bedroom. And the doors between must always be open for that is the way air currents flow: from kitchen, to bathroom, to bedroom, and if the doors are closed the heat builds up in the kitchen while the bedroom is cold. If I walked into another house and saw a bathroom door open to the kitchen I would be a little surprised, but here I never notice it.

Closets are a real poser. I can see why so many old houses had hall trees in them. Closets and cupboards built against a wall may be the answer in some cases, but not often. A roomy attic has helped solve the problem for us.

Often there is a wish to enlarge what was known as the front room or parlor. We added the former birthing room to ours, making a living room of comfortable size.

Upstairs the problem was again to find space for a bathroom. For years we had none up there, and reliance was on the chamber pot or "convenience" as it is known around here, or "thunder mug." Eventually we put a half bath in a hallway connecting the landing with the attic. Our guests were appreciative.

Let me offer a word here about guests' accommodations. At one time when the family was young, and at the other end quite old, I could put up eight or ten people by giving the old folks a proper bedroom upstairs, making the second room up there into a dormitory, and adding beds to the attic in the house and also over the woodshed. Then the old folks stepped out, the children grew up, and I gradually concentrated accommodations until I now have one guest room, and that is it. The dormitory has become my study again and the attics are real attics.

Attics are indispensable for the purposes assigned to them. They collect things, all kinds of things. I know an attic that became so full that one could no longer enter it. One went to the head of the stairs and tossed things over the barricade of accumulated treasure.

But the more order you can manage in the attic, the more it will hold. We have two attics, one in the house and one over the adjoining shed, the latter for rough stuff like tools, boards that might become useful, trunks, and household items no longer in use. The house attic holds clothing not in daily use (in garment bags), a wardrobe, a few trunks, hand luggage, some furniture, and extra books of our own authorship. It also holds a couple of trunks full of rather battered silver that is not suitable in a country home where dining is in a kitchen and the dining table is used for all sorts of purposes, including cutting up the carcass of a pig or side of beef.

As for chimneys, sometimes these are built in, as ours in the brick part are. They are old and lack flue liners. Because they are not safe, we use them with care and have them cleaned regularly. New chimneys, having flue liners and clean-outs at their base, are much safer. Even in one of these a fire is a scary thing, however, and flue liners do develop cracks and gaps. In some old houses the chimney is short, resting on a wooden framework six- or eight-feet high, upstairs or in the kitchen—not recommended. In some very old houses the chimney is of stone or of stone and brick. It sits in the middle of the house with a fireplace on three sides. The main fireplace is or was for cooking, with a crane, ovens, and also a special space to hold a big tub for heating water. Unfortunately, when stoves replaced the fireplaces, many of these old chimneys were removed and the space given over to closets. A small chimney replaced the big old one, and more is the pity. It is true that these chimneys are no longer useful, but they were pleasing to look at and sit by.

Then there is the matter of water. The prudent purchaser will want to be sure of its presence, quantity, quality, and dependability before concluding a deal to buy property. The more naive, among whom we count ourselves, will be so overcome with having found the right place that the mere matter of a proper supply of water will be incidental.

When we took possession of our place, I asked a neighbor how to turn on the water. He offered to show us. In a corner of the kitchen he took up a loose floorboard. Under it was a hole in the ground with pipes showing. Our neighbor took a cork out of a half-inch lead pipe, stanched the flow of water with his thumb, drew it to a similar pipe that penetrated the house, and bound the two together with friction tape. That was it. The water was from an old spring on the hillside above the house, and the only pressure was from the force of gravity.

Half a century ago this was enough water to supply two households and the barn. With no bathrooms, tubs, showers, or automatic washers, a pitcher and bowl served for the body, a pan for the dishes, and two laundry tubs plus a hand wringer were set up in the kitchen. One changed clothing once a week and bedding once a month. Today, to wear the same underwear two days in a row is an imposition. So we have washers, tubs, and showers in addition to ordinary plumbing.

Under these modern conditions, few natural springs are fully adequate. Our own spring is pretty good but not infallible. For two or three years we experimented with increasing its flow and then gave up. Now we have a dual water system: The spring water comes into the house but is used only for drinking and cooking. Water pumped up from the pond serves all other household purposes, including the bathrooms and the washers. The spring would run dry now and then, in which case we brought drinking water from a neighbor. But since Marshall has planted some two hundred thousand evergreens on the hillside above the spring, thus preventing surface runoff and enhancing the water table, the water flows steadily most of the time.

Many other country people have solved their water problems by installing artesian or driven wells. In a very dry year even some of these fall pretty low, but in general they serve well. A few lucky people have so heavy a flow from their springs that their needs are satisfied on a permanent basis.

A home in the country is no good without a shed, or indeed, several sheds. If you burn wood, and of course you will, a season's supply will take a lot of space—several cords worth. It is best if such a shed is attached to the house so that wood can be brought in without putting on an extra layer of clothing in cold weather. There must also be a place for a bench and tools. And for the family car. And for lawn mowers and garden tools. How these areas are handled depends on the layout, but the overall space must be large.

Finally there is the matter of the roof. If it is sound, so much the better. If it needs replacing, do it now, for it may be a long time before you get to it again. Be sure the flashing around the chimneys and in the valleys extends some distance under the shingles. Eaves are a special problem; there must be a shield, preferably of aluminum, extending a foot or more up under the shingles along them. In winter, snow on the roof will melt during the day, flow down along the valleys to the eaves, and then freeze at night, forming a dam of ice. This dam collects the melting snow the following day, and the water so collected will seep in under the shingles, causing a leak inside the house. This is called setback. Once water begins to drip inside the house it is almost impossible to locate where it comes in, for it may come in on a rafter or flow down the rafter to a lower point before penetrating the house. And the more heat that is allowed to escape from the house through the roof, the more likely it is that leaks of this kind occur. A metal shield under the shingles, in the valleys, and along the eaves will help.

As for gutters, it is best to forget about them. They may be useful in good weather, but as soon as snow collects on the roof and is either raked or slides off of its own accord, off come the gutters. A lost cause.

In the course of restoration, you may find that you want to make additions to your house—an extension here, a whole room there. A most interesting and exciting enterprise. Once you have your plans, and I hope you make them yourself without the impersonal help of an architect, then with local labor you can achieve just what you want. And help to do it yourself, too. That makes the house even more your own, and you and the home will both respond, with yet another bond between you.

3

Keep It Simple

THE BASIC RULE IN FURNISHING A COUNTRY HOME IS: KEEP IT simple. Thoreau said it many times. Simplify, simplify. And he was right. Only he didn't know how right he was because he couldn't foresee the complications of life in a technological age.

If you simplify your own life today, it will still be far more complicated than Thoreau ever dreamed of. Still, the basic rule will work, assuming the first steps have been taken: That you have decided to change your life-style from the flatness and frustration of the city or the suburbs. That you have found a part of the country that means something, an area that you really enjoy. That you have found just the right house and it is about to become your home ground.

Furnishing it will depend on what you already have, a lot of which may be unsuitable to new surroundings. Some of your belongings can be adapted with a little imagination and ingenuity. But if you ignore the need to keep things simple, you are in big trouble.

There are two ways of making your decisions here. It is a little like packing for a trip. You can go through your wardrobe looking for what you might need. This dress or those shoes or that sports jacket might be useful, and perhaps a dress, coat, or dark suit to wear at the theater. By

21

this method you wind up with at least one extra suitcase that will be a burden to you wherever you go. In these days of few porters, to pack more than you can handle yourself is a mistake.

Some people simply pack up everything in their city or suburban home and move it by van, or even two vans, to the new location. But they will find, when they get to the new place, that it would have been a good idea to make a deal with the van company to return in, say, six months, and take everything back to the city.

If, on the other hand, you sort rigorously and discard, give away, or sell at a lawn sale that which will not be needed in your country home, you might end up with only one van load, the price of moving will be much less, and you won't have to make that deal for the return trip six months later.

What about those items that would be less than useful in your new surroundings but of which you are very fond? Take them along and store them in the barn, if there is one (and there should be). In the course of time this surplus will grow until the children are old enough to start their own homes. The barn will be an immediate source of help to them, and the supply will soon be exhausted to a good purpose.

When you start to sort things out, I suppose your decisions come down to your basic set of mind. Do you think you really do have a use for all these things? Or do you have a more or less unconscious wish to continue your urban values in the country? Can you scrub out all these needs and values that have become habit, and start with a clean slate and a fresh mind open to new ideas and values? It may require a deliberate effort to take a new look at old things, to pass over the matching drapes and bedspreads, the dainty curtains, the electric frying pan, the clothes dryer for which you will have no need.

I stress this sorting-out process for two reasons. The

first is psychological. Possessions are the chains, sometimes remarkably resistant, that bind one to a place, a
structure of life, a round of daily habit, an unconscious
sense of behavior and responsibility that fits in well with
your urban environment, but not with the new one. A
definite break, a thoughtful and rational one, will help to
make the transition. There is the story of the woman who
always cut her pot roast in half before cooking it. Why?
Because that is how her mother did it. Why did her mother
do it? Because her pot was too small. That initial fact had
been lost to sight, but the habit lingered on.

The second reason for the sorting-our process is
practical. Many things seem natural in the city. A large
refrigerator, for example, is accepted under the guidance
of advertisers, or is considered a must. But it takes up a lot
of room, consumes more energy than a small one,
contains an across-the-top freezing unit that is superfluous
when you also have a freezer. A large refrigerator also
promotes the keeping of leftovers that you don't need.

Today's household accumulates dozens of small electrical appliances that are useless in a country home, unless
you plan deliberately to use them instead of the stove or
the eggbeater. If you bring them with you, plan some
storage space in the attic. You won't need them. A clothes
dryer in the country is ridiculous and uses expensive
energy. In any case, clothes dried in a dryer cannot equal
the fragrance of clothes dried in the sun, a fragrance that
makes you want to bury your nose in the armful that you
bring in from the line behind the house.

Fancy floor covering demands the vacuum cleaner or
the waxer more often than plain floors. Fancy antiques are
a nuisance if they must be cleaned and polished regularly.
Old furniture that is used to being battered is a different
matter. Old chests, desks, and tables combine readily with
modern types and are easier to live with than chairs and
couches whose fancy upholstery has to be preserved.

For Marshall and me the transition was easy. We had just been married, the second time for both of us, and we were unencumbered with possessions. We could and did start pretty much from scratch. There was no psychological break, only a new beginning, and everything was positive. A home, however, by its very permanence seems to acquire things, from family, auctions, travel, gifts, and temporary living quarters elsewhere. Our home was soon far from the bare rooms with which we started.

I hope your home has a very large kitchen. Ours started that way, a room of about twenty feet square. Later we enlarged it. Now it is some thirty-five feet square, and not a square foot too large.

The reason for a large kitchen is that it is the center of family activity. If it is small, there will always be some person, or perhaps some animal, in your way. For another thing, it is easier to have your meals in the kitchen instead of using a separate dining room. A dining room is one more room to care for; it often becomes a mere passageway between kitchen and living room. Family meals seem to occur naturally in the kitchen.

The kitchen is the work center of the house, from which all other household activities radiate. It is here that the baby sits in the high chair, and here that grandma sits in her rocker by the window—when she isn't doing her share of the housework. And she likes housework, too, even if it is only caring for houseplants, washing dishes, and caring for her own room.

In our kitchen, the big, old, cast iron, wood-burning cook stove, against a partial partition separating the utility room from the rest is, almost, the center of the entire house.

I stress that this is a wood-burning stove. In addition to its usefulness as a cooking device, such a stove seems to have a personality of its own, a spirit, one might say—an aura that embraces the whole family. It not only cooks food but also provides warmth and hot water. It keeps a steaming teakettle on the boil for that occasional cup of coffee or tea and provides steam that moisturizes the air, making it comfortable for people and houseplants. Country lore says that houseplants thrive best in a country kitchen where the steam from the kettle keeps the air just right. Incidentally, another bit of country lore is that houseplants started from a slip *stolen* from someone else's plant always thrive better than those legitimately acquired. My mother used to come home from the house of a friend with several slips acquired by illegal means, and she swore they always did well. I should add that the ability to steal slips from her friends houseplants, plus an unconquerable urge to deceive customs inspectors, were her only dishonesties.

An additional advantage of a wood-burning stove is having to keep it in fuel. To go out into the forest to cut down trees, work them up into proper lengths, split them, haul them to the shed, stack them, and then bring them into the house, gives one a lot of exercise of a kind most people enjoy. Somewhere in this process the wood is aged so as to burn hot and clean. At the end of the line, there are the ashes to be removed from the stove and spread on the gardens, sparingly, and on the lawns, copiously. If there is any clover in your lawn, ashes will bring it out.

One thing that prevents this exercise from being boring is that the results are so visible. A well-stocked woodshed is a beautiful thing—each row of wood, be it stove, chunk, or fireplace wood, is like money in the bank. And when one calculates the price of oil, gas, or electricity in the place of wood, it just about is. Moreover, heat from an organic source is known to produce negative ions in the air, creating a feeling of relaxed warmth. Conversely, heat from an inorganic source, such as electricity, creates positive ions that make one feel on edge, irritable, and snappish.

Flanking our cook stove are the counters and the sink—an old cast iron number that threatens to rust out but never has. In it are two dishpans and between them a bucket into which spring water for drinking constantly flows. Above the bucket hangs a tin dipper, a hard thing to locate these days but which can be found in some old country general stores. The separate water system for household purposes (pumped up from the pond at the foot of the garden) also serves the kitchen sink and washers.

When electricity became available we enclosed the original small woodshed to make a utility room and built on a really big woodshed. The utility room became part of the kitchen, separated by a partial partition. Though not large, it contains the clothes washer, refrigerator, a utility table, three wood boxes, and three cupboards. Obviously no space is lost.

A few years later when we finally took up permanent residence here, we enlarged the kitchen by what we now call the bay. Its main feature is a twelve-foot bay window looking out over the gardens, lawn, and pond. Placed inside it is an equally long plant table made from a board cut out of our own forest. The houseplants find it to be a natural habitat, and some of them have lived there for more than twenty years. The main part of the bay sitting area is some sixteen feet by twenty feet, with ceiling-high bookcases at one end. A professor's house seems to breed books. "I don't know what books do at night," a visitor of ours once remarked, "but they certainly do multiply awfully fast." Without shelves they become monsters leering at you from chairs and tables and the floor. The whole of the bay area is a step down from the kitchen and wide open to it. The dining table is just above the step.

Second in importance in this country kitchen only to the cook stove, is this dining table: a big, old harvest table that temporarily holds everything that comes into the kitchen except the firewood. In addition to the accouterments of dining, it also holds papers, that is, anything made of paper, such as newspapers, correspondence, reports, packages—all that snowstorm of paper that penetrates houses. And worse yet, they stay there until I make a determined effort to have them cleared away. I used to do that job, but since losing my sight several years ago, I have to make a nuisance of myself until someone else, meaning my husband, does the job with what grace he can manage to summon.

The center of this table is occupied by a very large lazy Susan, which holds condiments, pickles, jams and jellies, butter, honey, and even papers of special importance such as bank statements and memorandums concerning matters of immediate action. It also holds birthday and anniversary cards for a few days only.

Also kept on the table is a special little basket of my husband's incidentals and items from his pockets. The contents of it include his watch when he is not working, his extra glasses, his date book, his wallet, his pipes, and even memorandum slips, although these are illegal in that collection.

Without moving the table we can seat seven people. By moving it away from the step to the bay, another three people can be added. Made of old wood it will and does take all kinds of abuse, and I have long since ceased to use table linen or even hard mats. A good thing, too, for I find that table manners in a country kitchen are far from the conventional kind practiced elsewhere. There is a freedom here that is more compatible with the manners of Henry the Eighth than with those of Amy Vanderbilt.

Also to show how the old and the very old can agree, I use antique Canton dinnerware on this table. The china came to me from a great grandmother, who must have had a sea captain in her family. Much of it is chipped, some mended, and I die a little each time I damage or lose a piece. But I like it so much that I decided to get the use of it while I can. No one coming after me will feel about it as I do anyhow.

One of the most important aspects of this kitchen is what one does not see in it: an electric frying pan, an electric mixer (although I do have one in hiding), a blender (it is on a high shelf that I seldom reach). I have never had a microwave oven, because I don't need it with the wood-burning stove going all the time. In a cupboard are some emergency appliances to use when the stove is temporarily cold: a toaster, a teakettle, and a two-burner electric hot plate. Someone once gave me an electric knife; I hung it beside the knife rack but it gathered dust so I gave it to a rummage sale.

I don't know just how many other appliances are available today, probably a great many from bun warmers to hot dog cookers. But I suggest that they all be considered with a critical eye before they are lugged from the city to a country kitchen. And if you do bring them with you, I suggest that you look at them again and then perhaps donate them to the nearest good cause.

I have said that our kitchen stove provides all of our hot water for free, and so it does. It was not always so, for at the outset our only sources of hot water were the teakettle and a reservoir that was part of the stove. The present stove has a so-called water front, a hollow cast iron insert in the firebox that is connected by incoming and outgoing pipes to a hot water tank in the utility room. Cold water comes into this tank, which holds thirty-five gallons, circulates through the stove, returns to the tank, and recirculates so long as the fire is going. Since the fire is always going during the day, even in summer, this smallish tank takes care of our daily requirement of two loads of dishes, one load of laundry, incidental sink use, and three or four showers in the afternoon. All for free. When I hear how much other people spend on hot water, to say nothing of the cost of an electric stove for all cooking, I tend to feel just a little complacent about my old cast iron friend in the kitchen. A nasty attitude, I agree.

Opening out from this extended kitchen is the living room, a quiet place with a chunk stove and a fireplace, couch, desk, bookcases, and music. Separated from the living room by the hall is the master bedroom. Upstairs, one front room is the guest room and the other is my study. A half bath and attics go forth in a kind of tail and all are fully occupied.

After so many years here we do not feel any hardship from the internal arrangements in the house. They exactly suit us. Having been brought up with a sleeping porch, I would like one, but we can find no place for such a thing without cutting down a lovely, old wild apple tree that serves no good purpose except to flood that side of the house with blossoms each spring. We prefer the apple tree to the porch. We would also like a dressing room on the English model but can't supply it without depriving the north side of the kitchen of light. The light is more important to us than the extra space.

When we needed more study space we built a separate building up above a retaining wall that supports the woodshed. It is a saltbox nearly thirty feet long, full of desks, bookcases, a couch, an easy chair and a fireplace— also files and typewriters. The clatter of our typewriters never bothered us, each of us being absorbed in our own thoughts and compositions. But now that I use a recorder, the sound of a voice is something else again, so I have returned to the original study in the main house. A delightful arrangement.

When a house becomes a home it provides a kind of protective coloration for its inhabitants—an embrace. And when this happens, *here* has been realized. Or anyway, that is how we find it.

4

A Bowl of Cherries

HAVING BOUGHT, RESTORED, AND FURNISHED YOUR HOUSE, you might think that you can now sit back and enjoy it. Not so; or only partially so, for the art of restoration shades off into the ongoing chore of maintenance. If maintenance occurs as needed there is no problem. If it is delayed, additional needs accumulate at what becomes an alarming rate.

A house has life, too, and it resents having to live alone. A house seems to have an inner energy that ceases when left to itself. It has an innate compulsion to deteriorate when left to its own devices. For a period of some ten years, for example, our house was left without its family for at least one semester each year. And part of each semester occurs in cold weather. A number of times we have come home in mid-winter to find the wall behind the bathroom shower uneven and buckled instead of flat, and tiles popping. We also found accumulations of decay here and there, which seemed to vanish as we reestablished our residence. Often on entering the house for the first time in several months I would be struck by how shabby it was. Then either the shabbiness disappeared or I become used to it again, because I ceased to be aware of it.

That a house has a life of its own and needs constant maintenance to keep it alive was forcibly demonstrated to me by the fate of a neighbor's house that we had bought along with the property adjacent to ours. We wanted the land when it became available, but not the house which we knew to be a shambles. It had once been a small house, to which a very large new addition had been built on. The addition was on feeble foundations, which were crumbling. There was some doubt as to whether the house was hanging on the chimney or resting on the furnace, a large wood-burning affair in the cellar. When the house became vacant we removed all useful parts, such as doors, shelves, and windows. Then one clear day in winter, with snow on the ground for safety's sake, we poured gasoline on the floor and touched a match to it. I say we. Marshall and a neighbor did the job. I was squeamish and stayed at our house, watching from the kitchen window. I saw the blaze as the flames leapt through the old timbers and siding, and almost literally heard the screams of pain that came to me from an old house in agony. I was in a kind of agony myself. But after a few moments the feeling left me and I realized that the house was dead. So then I walked the quarter mile uphill to where the old house had stood and watched the last of the flames as they consumed the debris in the cellar hole. When the season changed we had a bulldozer fill in the old cellar hole, which today is still surrounded by the lilac and snowball bushes that had once given the old house some of its dignity.

So I stress the need for ongoing vigilance in the matter of maintenance. This means paint, inside but especially outside; attention to foundations, roofs, chimneys, beams, and rafters; and many smaller things like hinges, locks, plumbing, wiring, and floors.

An example of what I mean occurred one early spring day redolent with melting snow in the bright sunshine. I was working on a manuscript in the study, and Marhsall was splitting wood in the shed below. He came to the study for a moment of rest, sat in an armchair, and promptly noticed a leak in the low side of the sloping ceiling. The drip was just missing a row of bookshelves. Marshall sighed as he got up. "Life is just a bowl of cherries," he remarked as he returned to the shed to fetch a shovel. Then he cleared the snow off the back side of the roof. We had neglected to do it when we should have. It was a piece of routine maintenance. Had it gone any further we would have had some wet books. And if it happened often enough, that side of the study would have ended up with a good deal of rotting lumber.

Foundations should be inspected from time to time. Odd things can happen here: falling mortar, rotting sills, sags from too much moisture or standing water. Beams sometimes are host to powder post beetles, betrayed by small holes in them and tiny piles of fine sawdust under them. This little insect eats out the center of the beam but leaves the outside intact, except for the telltale pinholes. A spray takes care of them, but drive a knife blade into the beam to test for inner strength.

Regular outside paint is a must, every four or five years in some places, depending on the climate. This is especially so for window frames and the windows themselves, where putty dries out, falls off, and must be renewed. Paint helps to preserve the putty. This goes for storm windows, too.

Then, there is the essential matter of chimneys, especially if you burn wood. Such chimneys tend to collect creosote, a highly flammable material that is hard to remove except by burning. And in an old chimney above all others, burning must not be allowed to happen. It is bad enough in a modern chimney which always has a tile flue liner. An old chimney does not, and a fire in one of these can easily be a disaster. Old bricks are crumbly, and no one who has not seen, and heard, a chimney fire can have any idea how hot a chimney can get.

Creosote collects in a chimney through the burning of

anything that is damp. Green wood, for example, will do the job very well. The uninitiated tend to dump things in the stove firebox, such as wet paper towels or napkins, vegetable parings—if these are not more properly reserved for the compost heap. A milk carton seems innocuous; And so it is, if the inside is dry. A kettle boiling over also produces moisture that combines with wood smoke to make creosote. All no's.

Then there is the matter of plastic, which today surrounds us, as containers of all kinds are now made of it. I used to burn it in the cook stove as a matter of convenience. After a while, the stove started to smoke. I cleaned; it still smoked. It seemed to have no draft. I fussed over it for a while, and then Marshall inspected the chimney. A skin of plastic had formed over the inside of the flue about half way up, and it took a lot of banging with a heavy chain to dislodge it. The plastic I had been burning had vaporized up the chimney to the place where the heat was less, and at that point it had solidified. The first thin skin collected more and more until a large barrier had formed. I no longer burn plastic in the stove, and the chimney remains clear.

A regularly maintained chimney needs cleaning at least once a year. The local fire department will do it, usually in the early fall, for a fee. Or a professional chimney sweep will do it, if there is one in your vicinity. But you can do it yourself. A small evergreen tree inserted upside down through the top of the chimney (there should be a clean-out opening at its base) and pulled up by a rope from the bottom will do the job. A rope should be attached to the top end, too, in case the evergreen gets stuck.

Or instead of an evergreen, you can use a length of rolled up chicken wire; or a number of large chains on the end of a rope, raised and lowered and banged against the sides of the flue; or any other similar instrument of your own devising. Several are now manufactured for the purpose and can be bought at the local hardware store.

I have heard that in Ireland a live goose was once used as a preferred instrument. Tied to a rope, it was inserted into the chimney on the theory that its flapping wings would dislodge the soot. What was never finally decided, it seems, was whether the goose should be lowered into the chimney head first or feet first. In either case, it wound up on the family dinner table. And the chimney was at least cleaner that it was before.

Stovepipes also must be cleaned regularly. When in constant use, this means every three months. They must be taken down *and out*, and emptied into a bucket in the shed. Then the inside of the pipe must be scraped with an instrument, with special attention to the elbows. A trowel does fine.

If creosote has accumulated, the pipes should be burned out. They should be taken to the road, where the danger of setting a fire is reduced. With one end toward the wind, the other end is lifted slightly, and a half a sheet of newsprint is placed just inside the mouth of the pipe. After a splash of kerosene, a match is touched to the paper, and one stands guard. The roar of the flames tells what might happen in the house if the pipes caught fire there. When they are cool, the pipes are emptied, and it is astonishing to see what comes out.

If a chimney fire does occur in your house, be sure to take the pipes down afterwards and empty them, or you will have no draft. If you always burn only dry wood, you may never have to burn out the creosote.

Finally for outside maintenance, there is the roof. If it is new it may last for a long time. I was surprised to find that in our case, the roof on the south side of the house deteriorated faster than that on the north side. I suppose it is the effect of greater melting in the sun and freezing at night. In any case, a roof may have to be renewed only in sections. But a broken shingle here and there will spread and should not be neglected, especially if there is something inside the house that can be damaged by water (and there always is, including beams and rafters).

In addition to stoves and stovepipes, indoor maintenance involves plumbing, wiring, and redecorating. Ceilings, walls, and floors must be repainted from time to time, if that is how you have finished them. Wallpaper, if you use it, must be renewed occasionally.

As for floors, I counsel against wax or any other top dressing that has to be periodically stripped and reapplied. In a country house shiny floors are nice but hard to keep up, for traffic is heavy even with a small family. Floors must be refinished if that is how you have decided to treat them. But if you choose not to use a fancy finish, you will soon get used to the resulting shabbiness and live comfortably with what surrounds you. Try using flower arrangements here and there in season. They make the shabbiness look homelike.

Plumbing is a different matter. If something goes wrong with it you will know it at once, and here there is no temporizing. A frozen water pipe, a faulty toilet, or a plugged drain will put your system out of order until it can be fixed. One can always pee in the shed in case of emergency, or take a walk up to the pasture, but this can be a considerable inconvenience as well as a discomfort when there is a foot of snow on the ground.

Frozen water pipes can be thawed by the application of heat, depending on the location. Anything from a blow torch to a hot water bag will do the job. To keep the pipes from freezing again they can be insulated or wrapped with a thermal tape plugged into an electrical outlet; or the water can be left turned on just a little to keep it moving in the pipes in cold weather. This is especially true for spring water. Pump water is a different matter because the pump is pretty active most of the time.

A plugged toilet can usually be relieved by use of a plunger. Failing that, strong measures may mean a good deal of expert help, including that of a professional plumber, if there is one on whom you can call.

As for the drain, this also may only require a solvent poured down the sink or the toilet, or it may mean something better. Once when we had such an emergency I consulted the local plumber. He served in the hardware store and did not have the time for much in the way of house calls, so he lent me what was needed: a string of a dozen ten-foot lengths of steel rods, hinged together. I was at home alone at the time. I carted them home, down to the cellar, and inserted the whole string from the clean-out opening of the drain down to the cesspool. Whatever was wrong—sometimes it is the roots from a tree or shrubs that penetrate the pipe at its joints—cleared up. But it was some time before I could bring myself to pick up those rods and return them to my friend.

Electrical wiring is something else again. Here the improvised approach to a problem is to be avoided at all costs. Professional skill is necessary here, for anything less can be a disaster. A small neglect can cause a big fire and is not worth the risk. You may have to wait your turn for help, but wait. If you are a professional electrician yourself, well and good. But be sure you know what you are doing.

Finally in the matter of maintenance, there is a yearly operation that occurs outside for the benefit of the inside. It is called banking, but not the kind you do in connection with your checking account, although it has its effect there, too.

Old country houses are not all that tight around the

foundations, and in cold weather a lot of frost can penetrate the house from that source. The traditional remedy is to bank the house for the winter. It is best done by the middle of the fall so as to settle and be in place by the time snow flies.

The method is to apply plastic sheeting from a roll of maybe three-foot material: a foot of it on the ground and two feet or more up the side of the house, and tacked in place. Then you apply old hay that some farmer has discarded or that you have saved yourself for this purpose. Break the bales and apply the hay around the whole house, some three feet or more in height against the house walls. It will settle so use plenty. Next, go into the forest and cut evergreen boughs. Lay these on top of the hay to keep it from blowing and to add insulation—also for aesthetic reasons. When our house is treated this way it looks like it is sitting in its own Christmas wreath. One year I put a huge red bow on the wreath at the front door, which is permanently closed at this time of year. The difference in warmth that this banking makes inside the house is immediately noticeable, even on a cold, windy day.

Maintenance needs such as these constitute our bowl of cherries. That bowl has remained pretty constant in all the years we have lived here. With more skill than we possess, your bowl may be a smaller one. But there will always be one or two cherries in the bottom of it, and you may even come to welcome them as part of the challenge to your ingenuity and skills. What tasks you can cope with successfully help tell you who you are, and sharpen your sense of identity. You may not be aware of this at the time, but eventually you will, and will like the result.

5

Mobility

IN THE CITY OR SUBURBS MOBILITY IS LARGELY A MATTER OF getting around, usually by car, on paved streets and highways.

It is that way in the country, too, but that is only part of it. For one thing, country roads, where unpaved or ungraveled, are of dirt or of a mixture of dirt and gravel. The surface varies greatly from one season to another. In summer such country roads are pretty and lovely to travel, taking you into odd places that the person who stays on paved highways never sees. By fall such roads are washboards. In winter, they are again good if the snowplow has done its proper job. They are smoother then than in summer and hard, if frozen. However, a melting day or a rain in winter will coat such roads with wet snow that freezes at night and keeps you off them the next day. I have seen the whole state of Vermont covered with half an inch of ice. Schools were closed, and you could call anyone on the phone and be sure to find him or her at home.

The big season for country roads around here, and doubtless in other parts of the country as well, is spring. Since the roads have been plowed in winter, the frost has had a chance to go deep. Four feet is usual, and it has been known to go twice as deep as that. The frost comes out slowly as the weather moderates, and where no gravel has been applied the surface of the road turns to mush, a kind of jelly that even quivers in certain spots. If you live near one of these roads you take your precautions. Unless you have the proper kind of rig, you stay away from them in a car, or you walk.

Ruts form on country roads in spring, sometimes axle-deep. For some reason or other the ruts are always crooked, and if you try to travel them with any speed, they will throw you onto the shoulder, if there is one, or against a bank or into a ditch. Just a little extra speed will do the job quite well. So take it easy. Eventually the frost is all out and the ruts are smoothed over by the grader, which has a great time messing up the surface, catching on subsurface rocks and pulling them up and onto the road. The result is a shaggy surface that time and traffic compact, so that eventually a pretty good surface is achieved, but more by nature and use than by the hands of humans.

Around us most back roads have been treated with truckloads of gravel over the years and are much less treacherous than they used to be. Some still have grass growing down the middle and are to be avoided at all costs in the spring mud season. No gravel there. Even gravel roads can be washed-out by heavy rains and become virtually impassable. A certain spot near us is well-known for having a stream running beneath it in spring, and not through a culvert. Those who travel past there watch for a certain hole, some two feet deep, that opens up to engulf the unwary. The first passerby who notices this phenomenon places a long stick in it, warning the neighbors that a familiar hazard has again shown itself. Someone telephones the town manager, who sends a truckload of gravel to the spot. That usually fixes it, for that season at any rate.

So where is your house? On a paved road, a paved

back road, a graveled back road, or a dirt back-back road? The instinct of many city people is to get as far away from the crowd as they can, and they often end up on a back-back road. Whatever your location, it will determine the kind of vehicle, or vehicles, you drive.

But passenger transportation is not the only mobility you must plan for. Loads also must be accommodated. A bag of cement or two, pieces of lumber, feed and grain for animals, bales of hay, bits of machinery, and loads of wood, are just a few. Then there are jobs to be done around the place, like fencing, meaning that you must transport fence posts and wire to where they are needed, perhaps at the head of a stony and hilly pasture. Trash to be taken to the dump; and bushels of apples to be brought in from the orchard; and a beef or pork carcass to be taken to the locker; and more and more. But perhaps none is so necessary as hauling wood. This means a rig that can be driven through the forest, with tools aboard—one that can be driven back out of the forest with a full load of firewood. In our area the forest floor is not the poet's delight of smooth earth and plushy moss. It is very rough indeed, with rocks and cavities where trees once stood but are now blown over and either sunken into the earth or used for wood. I am not comfortable in a rig crawling over such terrain, lurching and nearly tipping over (or so it seems to be), and I prefer to walk. But my swashbuckling husband is fearless in such circumstances, so maybe I am unduly chicken. So, given your own situation, what will be your choice of transport?

Fortunately, today there is a wide variety of multi-purpose vehicles. It was not so the year we decided to take up permanent residence. If you figure to get around a hundred percent by car, you might be right. But we did that and were a hundred percent wrong. If you live on a back road, or on a back-back road, a passenger car will serve pretty well for part of the year but not at all for most of the time. The roads are almost always rough in some places and very hard on front ends and shocks. A car whose natural habitat is a paved road rebels quickly on these rough ones, and the expense of maintenance can be high.

Our original choice was a used, eight-cylinder Olds sedan. It was an honest vehicle and it did its best. But it could not handle rough roads. Its front end was soon badly shaken. We could almost hear it panting as it put us down at our door. Also, its eight cylinders were too powerful, for too hard a touch on the accelerator, especially on a slippery surface, would cause it to lose traction and its wheels to spin. It would then have to be backed, precariously, to a spot where we could try again. Or else the car would stall in anguish, a state that matched our own emotions. In turns it would scrabble, lurching from side to side, and finally leap out onto the shoulder, if there was one, or more often into the ditch. Then it would stand exhausted as we sought to straighten it out. Once it dived headlong into a snowdrift that had come across the road, burying its front end and lifting its rear wheels off the road. There it stayed until the following morning when the snowplow had to remove it in order to accomplish its appointed task. Also, the plow driver obligingly had to drag it for nearly a quarter mile before it would consent to start, so cold had it become during the night. (Fortunately, it was close enough to home when it stalled for us to finish the trip on foot.) It had a blind side, too, being unable to back down a hill without finding a ditch on one side or the other into which to snuggle, a fatal kind of attraction.

After more than a year of this type of thing the car was exhausted and so were we. We turned it in on one of the first civilian Jeeps to be put on the market after World War II and since then we have never been without a Jeep. We now have two, one of them a workhorse and the other, a far cry from the hardier of its ancestors, good for little more than a passenger service.

A basic principle of life around here is to make do with what you have. If all you have is a Jeep, you make do with that, even if you have a number of children in the family. I once had two adults and five children in our original Jeep, but the present one will barely hold a total of five, and one of the five has to be slim indeed.

If you would combine passenger service with hauling and work in the woods, a four-wheel-drive pickup is about as versatile and satisfactory as you can get. Many of these combine work quality with passenger comfort and have become fashionable even among city folk. Alternatives are Jeeps (not all that comfortable) and Scout-type vehicles, which can be useful. Passenger cars also now come with a number of advantages for driving on bad roads: high- and low-range gears, four-wheel drive, front-wheel drive, and good clearance over rough roads. Some of these are still experimental and all are expensive. Quality is caveat emptor. If you have any mechanical ability and know-how in this area, now is the time to exercise it.

Perhaps you would have one of these heavy-duty passenger rigs and a tractor for work in the woods. If you do use a tractor you will have to have a trailer hitched to it for hauling equipment—saws, axes, cant hooks, wedges, extra fuel, a jug of drinking water, and the like—and for moving the wood once it has been worked up. We have never used a tractor and trailer in the woods, but we have used a Jeep and trailer and find it does well. A Jeep is sufficiently flexible to maneuver in tight places and is cheaper to operate than a tractor. And since we wouldn't use a tractor for any other purpose, including gardening, we don't own one. But we do sometimes use a neighbor's tractor if we have a particularly rough job to do, such as plowing up a portion of rocky pasture. Such assistance may be on a hire basis, on an exchange-of-work basis, or as a neighborly act. Neighbors around here are always willing to help greenhorns and seasoned country people alike, an they always come to each other's aid in times of emergency. If someone has had an accident, or is sick, or has lost a barn in a fire, the neighbors will do chores, milk cows, mend fences, and help in any necessary rebuilding until that person is on his or her feet again. Those who do such work may at some time need help themselves.

Many times we have been rescued by a neighbor after our car or Jeep has gotten stuck in mud or snow. Yes, a Jeep can indeed get stuck now and then, although more often now than in the early days when Jeeps were synonymous with all that was sturdy and relentless.

When a neighbor helps you out, however, there is always a tacit recognition that something is owed, as a matter of principle and also in the interests of individual independence. No matter what your neighbor does for you, or what you do for your neighbor, the final question is, "What do I owe you?" The answer may be a sum of money, but rarely. Or the answer may be, "t'ain't worth it." In the latter case both of you will make a mental note that a favor has been done and a return favor is owed.

One form of mobility has pretty well been taken care of without the attention of the rural householder, except in the form of taxes. This is the school bus. Once a rather haphazard arrangement around here, it has now been put on a firm basis in most communities. Either the bus passes your house or it stops at a nearby crossroads where it collects and later decants its load of children.

Now and then all forms of transportation fail and you must stay at home. You are snowed in and the plow will not get to your road until tomorrow. Or there has been a flash flood, as happened to us once, cutting us off fore and aft. It was several days before the road could be repaired. With a freezer full of food we had no need to go to town, so we relaxed and enjoyed our privacy. No school buses passed the house during those few days. In an emergency we could have driven to where the road was blocked, to be met by a vehicle on the other side. But there was no reason to worry and we didn't.

Having lived here a number of years now, we think of our road as an old friend. Here is where the Olds used to slide downhill, backwards, into a ditch hard against a stone cliff on the far side. Try to get chains on a rear wheel in those circumstances! But we learned to. Farther along is a spot that regularly turned into a slough when the frost was coming out. It is on a curve, which, when icy, would slew your rig into the ditch, with a brook just beyond it that almost jeered at your discomfort. And here is where a rail spur to the quarries once crossed the road. Rails and ties are now gone, but the stone foundations remained for years and presented the aspect of a stone wall to be surmounted by your car. Easy did it. There is the spot where a motorcycle smashed into a tree, nearly killing its riders. A little farther on, cowslips grow in a swampy area beside the road, offering some of the first spring greens for your table. On the lower road, wild leeks offer another succulent spring green, tasting faintly of garlic and mild onions. Streams cross under the road in several places, and on the first day of fishing those who understand such things know just where to park the car for a pleasant exploration with pole and bait.

A final requirement in the matter of mobility is to find, and then cherish, a mechanic who will advise you, repair your vehicle, come to your place if you can't get there, and charge you no more than is reasonable. Such a mechanic will save you many mistakes and solve many frustrations for you. You will become fast friends. And since it is not likely that you can ever do much of a favor in return, you will always be indebted to your mechanic.

6

Meat of the Land

NOW THAT YOU HAVE YOUR OWN HOME GROUND IN THE country with a substantial number of acres (I hope)—what will you do with it?

I find it hard to think of land as a possession, though I know plenty of people who do. To me, this is short-sighted. If the land does not actually own me (and I'm not so sure about that), I at least have the feeling that it looks to me as a trustee, to manage and protect it for the sake of the generations of those who will follow us here, on this piece of earth.

One could, of course, supply a little so-called benign neglect and let the land grow up to brush, then saplings, then in due course, trees. If properly managed, the land will provide the right kind of habitat for wild creatures: birds, small animals, and a few large animals. Around here we have deer, bear, and a kind of coyote. In other parts of the country the size and variety of fauna may be even greater.

In many parts of the country, however, much formerly fertile land has been abandoned, and it seems to be a pity to lose any more potentially useful farmland, even in marginal farming areas. This is not meant to encourage a leap into commercial farming, unless you have experience in that occupation or have inherited a going farm with a full set of stock, tools, and the capital needed for additional outlays, or at least a kitty of five hundred thousand dollars to invest in all of these many and very expensive items, from land to the last ball of twine.

And by tools I don't mean shovels, rakes, and hoes, or even simply plows and harrows. I mean gang plows and harrows, and the tractors to haul them. I also mean milking machines, barn cleaners and feeders, pumps, milk coolers, and cleaners, manure spreaders, bailers, choppers, field wagons, silos, silo loaders and unloaders, wagons, hoists, and many more in enormous variety, all costing an arm and a leg to purchase, and the other arm and leg to repair and maintain.

Then there are the seeds and the planters for each variety of crop, fertilizers, herbicides, pesticides, and again the spreaders that transfer these items from container, which may be the tank truck, to the ground. Life as a commercial farmer brings many rewards and means of fulfillment, but high income and leisure time are not among them. And if this kind of farming is your thing, both you and your family had better be of the same mind.

If you have only a moderate amount of land, however, the question of commercial farming is academic. Instead, the opportunity to engage in subsistence farming presents itself and, to my mind, is to be welcomed. For here lies adventure and satisfaction without too much frustration or financial outlay. Subsistence farming is to be embraced in all its variety and challenges, none of which are beyond the bounds of human endurance. Such farming can form the basis of a lasting home economy which becomes more rewarding as you pursue it. It can be expanded as your imagination and amibition grow. Or its practice can be reduced, if and when you find your time, energy, and enthusiasm on the wane.

46

To cite our own experience, Marshall and I were both greenhorns despite a certain amount of exposure to country life. We started with one hundred thirty-five acres and later added the adjoining farm of two hundred thirty acres. This gave us a hundred acres of tillage, all of it infertile, thin, suffering from long neglect, but not yet grown up to brush and saplings. It could be made productive if we moved fast enough. Both farms offered a good many acres of scrubby, stony, hilly pastureland of the sort left by a glacier scraping over it, leaving behind a layer of debris. The rest of the land was forested, forming the basis of a maple sugar operation, and was in fairly good shape.

As a first step we arranged to have a neighbor live in the cottage across the road and farm the land on a minimum basis. He would pay no rent and we would receive no share, but the purpose was to make a start on bringing the land back into production, to mend fences, enclose pastures, plow tillage, repair the barn, and eventually constitute a handy deduction on our income tax return. Both the federal and state tax authorities have scrutinized this arrangement with some ardor but have approved it.

This partnership paid off in land fertility and production, maintenance of barn and fences, and a large milking herd. And a major advantage in this arrangement is that our partner owns all of the equipment.

With the experienced guidance of the country forester, we have planted most of the scrub pasture to pine trees, which over the years have become a plantation of some two hundred thousand trees. Where once I picked wild berries under an open sky, I can now get lost in a forest of pines. The lower branches have been pruned so as to make for high-grade lumber when the trees are harvested, but at the base of the trees it is dark and still, and the heavy carpet of pine needles seems to generate a kind of peace and quiet in the dim light. Moreover, good ground cover holds the water, preventing flooding and runoff. Our spring, guarded by this new forest, no longer fails us in an especially dry summer.

Now deeply involved in subsistence farming, we expanded our talents as we went along. We have stored, canned, and frozen what we would need throughout the winter in order to become virtually self-sufficient in the matter of food. It is no longer true that we can get by spending a total of just fourteen dollars in one month for the few staples we require, as once we did in 1949, but the equivalent in terms of inflated dollars is still possible.

Our eventual goal was to own our own land without mortgage, to produce our own goods except staples, and to cut down to the very minimum on expenses for artificial energy. As our plan to live in the country developed and as we finally became free of our city selves to give the plan our full attention, it turned out to be much as we envisioned it when we bought the place just twenty-four hours after struggling up that muddy road for the first time. For better or for worse, but mostly better, it turned out to be our fortune, full of golden opportunities and adventure. Without realizing it, we were developing the kind of life-style that later became the goal of young people during the sixties and seventies.

There was a lot to learn. We experienced among other things the frustrations and satisfactions of producing our own meat: beef, veal, pork, lamb, poultry, rabbit, and kid. Incidentally, there was only one of the latter, and it tasted like strongly flavored lamb. We also tried some of the wild beasties, including squirrel, very good, and opossum, not so good. Someone told us that young woodchuck was tasty, but we tried it and disagreed. Porcupine was suggested. It was said to taste like chicken if you cooked it just right, but we resisted. Then, of course, there was venison, which, when taken out of season around here is called "rabbit." There is nothing better than "rabbit" chops, cooked over a camp fire and served with good bread and red wine. Make it a jug of red wine.

A neighbor of ours, a recent city man, once found that his garden was being ravaged by what turned out to be a big buck. So one day he took aim and fired at the critter. In his death throes, the buck leapt and caught his antlers in the branches of an apple tree—and hung there, in full view of the road. The neighbor got in his car and drove down to the home of another neighbor. "Bill," asked the man in trouble, "what do you know about 'rabbit'?" "Well," said Bill, a local product, "I know better at night." "But this is daylight," was the reply, "and this rabbit is hanging in plain sight." "Okay," said Bill, "we'll fix it." So Bill got out his pickup, put his tools in it, and laid a rifle beside the tools. "What's that for?" asked the neighbor. "Under these circumstances," explained Bill, "if I see a game warden, I lay a shot as close to him as I can." Within half an hour the "rabbit" was cut down, cleaned, and divided fifty-fifty, and not trace of the deed remained.

Then there is the domestic variety of meats, some of which turn out to be more trouble than they are worth, all of which we modified over time, in terms of labor. Lambs and calves could not be put out to pasture by themselves without expensive fencing, but had to be staked or tethered on the lawn, which meant faithful attention. And one of the lambs, silly creature, managed to hang itself by the neck on its rope. Tethering animals is good for the yard, and we have friends who regularly fatten their lambs by this means. But it takes time when time is short.

When laying hens pass their term of usefulness they can be dressed off and tucked into the freezer, if you don't mind cooking them later, long and carefully, full of herbs, in order to make them edible. Now we bury old hens and buy our poultry in the market. It is possible to raise birds for meat alone, dressing them off at four or five months of age. And they are good—if you don't mind the dressing off part. We have done it many times, but enough is now enough.

In the early days of butchering our own beef, we slaughtered and skinned off on the place, hung the carcass in the barn or cellar until the following day. We were careful to select a cool time of year, preferably November. Then we would cut the meat ourselves, quarter by quarter on the kitchen table. I would have the knife in one hand and the book in the other. Then we would wrap, label, and freeze the meat in our own big freezer. It worked, even though some of the cuts were a bit on the nonconforming side. We also found that no matter how close our relationship with the animal in question had been, once the head and hide were removed, it was just a carcass. It is a little different with a pig because the hide stays on, but one gets used to this, too.

Today the dressing and carving job is much easier because there are commercial services to do it. A slaughter-house will fetch the animal from your barn and take it away. After processing, wrapping, and freezing, you take home the meat packed neatly in cartons and store it in your freezer. We have found, however, that there are many opportunities for error, and you sometimes receive some-one else's beef instead of your own. By chance or otherwise the beef has been mixed up, and the substitutions are usually of inferior quality—which is how you know.

So now we have devised a system that is virtually foolproof. We slaughter on the place, courtesy of a skilled neighbor, and take the carcass to a private cooler for ten days or so for hanging; then we take it ourselves to the home of a meat cutter who works for a local supermarket. He has set up his own cutting facilities in the back of his garage. There he cuts it, and we wrap and mark it, then take it home or to a local commercial locker for freezing and storage.

For a number of years we produced our own pork, from piglet to pork chop. We had an enormous sow, almost six feet long. At the appropriate time we would take her to a neighbor's boar, and eventually she would produce maybe fourteen piglets. On the first occasion she farrowed, I acted as midwife, or pigwife as someone said. After that she proceeded on her own without help. When the piglets were six weeks of age we would sell them, keeping one or two for ourselves to raise and start all over again. That came to a lot of work, too, so we eventually consumed the sow (her hams weighed forty pounds) and thereafter bought piglets in the spring, raised them through the summer and fall. We would butcher on the place in November, cut and freeze the fresh meat, cure bacons and hams, and render lard, as well as make our own sausages flavored to our own taste.

My husband likes to raise piglets. They are so human in their responses to people! We had one, once, that would occasionally join us for a cookout, a short distance from his pen. Our pigs inhabit a former milk house known as the "Palais des Porcs." It has a good yard, shade, and something to play with, like an old basket or pail. Since pigs seem to do better in pairs, it is also possible to raise two and sell one to pay for the other. And you know you have good clean pork. We still do it this way.

Dressing off pork is easier than dressing off beef because the commercial slaughterhouses are less apt to get the pigs mixed up. Not so many of them, for one thing. And since only the hair is removed in processing, and the skin stays on, one is more easily apt to recognize a familiar black spot, color, or mixture thereof.

In short, having tried all of the alternatives, we have

now reduced our homegrown meat to beef and pork. We also have our own eggs, and through having a financial interest in our partner's milking herd, we have our own milk. By concentrating on these few items we have plenty of ongoing goodness, the backbone of our home-produced protein. By agreement, our partner takes care of our brood cow, who produces a calf a year for the freezer. There is annually one of her young approaching the dressing-off stage and another maturing for the following year.

We know what our animals have been fed. A calf drinks its mother's milk for the first few weeks, gradually gets onto hay, and then eats only hay and grass until about a month before butchering, when it is "fitted" for that event. This includes feeding the animal a gallon of vinegar over a period of three or four weeks. The vinegar is sprinkled daily over the grain ration and seems to be quite tasty. It tenderizes the meat on the hoof, so to speak. It really does work.

Venison, the only other meat we are now apt to home-produce, depends on the luck of the hunter. We do sometimes have it in the freezer, and we could have it more often if we paid more attention to the matter of getting it. But for one thing, the woods are so full of careless hunters during the legal season that a property owner is foolhardy indeed if he ventures into his own forest during those frantic days. We no longer get "rabbit," though we do sometimes share in someone else's. It is always tasty, and sharing is the means of spreading the guilt in case the warden comes around.

We were turned off, I think, from getting our own "rabbit" when one late afternoon Marshall went to an upper meadow where he knew a big buck came to graze in the evening. He took a gun up there along the edge of the woods, and stretched out in a small depression where he was so comfortable he feel asleep. Pretty soon the big buck came out of the woods and stood at the edge of the depression, calmly looking him over. Marshall, by now awake, stared back, unable to move until the buck turned and went quietly back into the woods. Marshall returned to the house, looking a little surprised and a little pleased, too, at what he had—and hadn't—done. And has not done, since that time.

You can produce meat on your land on a subsistence farming basis for just you and your family, or you can make it into a wider occupation with a salable surplus. Beef cattle can be just a small part of your overall enterprise or it can be extended according to the land available, the financial returns, and your family's satisfaction. The most important factor in this equation is the price of grain, which is much more costly than it used to be, especially for cattle. For pigs, a certain ingenuity may be useful. For instance, a man we know has an informal contract with a local school to pick up edible garbage, the leavings from the school lunch, for his pigs. The school kitchen has a special receptacle and does not mix inedible garbage with what goes to the pigs. It is assumed that if such food is good for children, surely it will be good for pigs. (Although I suspect that it wouldn't compare favorably to commercial pig feed from the standpoint of nutrition.)

Pigs will also relish surplus vegetables from the garden, as well as edible trimmings from vegetables and meat from the kitchen. I knew a woman who was required to keep a forty-quart milk can under her kitchen sink into which she dumped her dishwater for the pigs. Nothing wrong with that except the inconvenience. I do draw the line!

I keep two small garbage pails on the kitchen counter: one for the pigs and the other for the compost pile in the corner of the garden. This second one holds coffee grounds, tea leaves, and paper such as napkins and towels, for these are also biodegradable and constitute a good earth conditioner.

However, such ingenuity as this takes time and may not be worthwhile if there are other pressing jobs at hand. And if you work off the place for your main income, it is a chore.

Other animals that can be raised on a subsistence farm are rabbits, milk goats, and poultry, of course. These require a minimum amount of attention, and often there is a market for rabbit meat (real rabbit this time) and goat's milk and cheese. Bee keeping is another fairly easy enterprise once you get the hang of it—not only for the honey for which there is usually a good market, but also for the pollination function. Many orchardists rent a hive or two during the blossoming season in order to promote pollination.

If from this discussion you have gained the impression that to produce your own meat depends on your own priorities and facilities and on how much work you are prepared to undertake, then you are absolutely right. The same is true of all aspects of land management, from planting a forest to reclaiming fields, and from animal husbandry to kitchen gardening. Plainly, it must be the kind of work you enjoy. If it isn't, then don't try it for any longer than it takes to be sure. Without the pleasures and rewards reaped from work you like, laboring on the land is drudgery and no rationalization will make it anything else.

For ourselves the satisfactions have been rich indeed. I know who had the property rights to this good earth before we did, and I know how some of its owners cherished it and how others mistreated it. Falling into disuse, it had become rank and ragged. A little here and a little there, we have seen the need and supplied the means,

and I have felt the land react, a living, breathing thing—
meadow and pasture, forest and plantation—to become
productive and life-sustaining. We have put much of
ourselves into its care and have been rewarded, not only by
financial profit but also by friendship, by its response to
the hand that has loved it. We have been privileged to
bring it back into production, to experience the immense
satisfaction and sense of achievement of seeing it thrive—
and knowing that part of ourselves has been defined on it,
and by it.

7

Gardening

A VAST NUMBER OF BOOKS HAVE BEEN WRITTEN ABOUT GARDEN-ing, filling libraries and shelves. Seed catalogs fill the mail in January, and now increasingly in December or any time after Thanksgiving. They make fascinating reading, and one is easily persuaded to buy all kinds of exotic seeds and plants. Let your imagination fly happily, but use moderation in buying. There are plenty of new varieties coming along, which make it fun and profitable to experiment. Try not to order more than you can use; you won't succeed, but try anyway.

In a country life-style, gardening is as basic as the earth itself. If you don't have a garden, your food costs will be high, your food quality will be low, and your soul will have ragged edges. I know of no scientific inquiry into the subject but I do feel the connection between fingers and soil as I work the good earth. More than vibes, a real dynamic connection. As I tend the soil, the soil tends me.

With so many sources of information readily available, propounding all kinds of methods and schools of gardening, the focus of this chapter is something else. It is on gardening as an aspect of country life-style—plus some perceptions that might be useful. It tells how we have adapted to some of the gardening conditions that prevail where we live.

Eating from the garden begins in March. Carrots, beets, and parsnips have wintered over in the ground, under the snow, and constitute the first spring vegetables. Parsnips especially are best when they have been through a freezing period in the winter. They are built that way.

These vegetables were heavily mulched in the fall, with stakes driven into the ground to mark the beginning and end of each row. With two feet of snow on the ground, these markers save a lot of tramping around in search of rows. All during the winter, these vegetables can be dug as needed. (One year we dug our last carrot with a pickax, the mulch having been too thin.)

Other leftovers are kale and spinach, planted late in the preceding summer and heavily mulched in the fall. As the mulch is taken off in the spring, the plants grow like mad as though they could not wait to renew their cycle. They provide the first fresh salad, and nothing tastes better. We have frozen bushels of spinach from a half-dozen plants as early as May.

About the first week in April we begin to plant the new garden. On the site of an old shed we have filled in the foundation with earth, the result being a so-called platform garden. We manured it and mulched it until it is now a fertile spot, well-drained and exposed to the full sun. The good drainage makes the difference, for the soil is friable long before the regular garden reaches that state. In this plot go the first lettuce, scallions, carrots, and radishes, plus other seeds that we experiment with: spinach for salad among them. Very quickly this plot produces wonderful young salad greens two inches tall. Thinnings from these rows can be eaten roots and all.

Soon edible wild plants come into production. Dandelion greens, tender and tasty before the blossoms appear; wild milkweed, the tender top few leaves and also the blossoms; cowslips; fiddlehead ferns; lamb's quarters, a delicious green; wild leeks, growing in thick clumps.

In the domestic garden, the rhubarb is showing by April, and when the stalks reach three or four inches they can be pulled, the leaves discarded—they contain oxalic acid and are poisonous. The stalks are stewed slowly in their own juice on the back of the stove. Add a little sugar—we have tried honey and also maple syrup but white sugar, shame on us, seems the tastiest. A uniquely delicious dish.

In the domestic garden, the asparagus comes on in May. The most ferocious human appetite for asparagus is eventually satisfied by late June, so we freeze the surplus and stop cutting on July Fourth, a traditional date for that operation.

Garlic is an interesting perennial, for it sows itself in two ways: it propagates both by the cloves and by seeds. And it should be in a permanent bed unless you need that space for something else. To start, break apart a bulb of garlic and plant the cloves some six inches apart. When the shoots appear they will be slender and green and can be picked, one or two from a plant, and used in salads as chives for a delicate flavor. As the plants mature, some will send up a sturdy stalk, at the top of which will appear seeds in a round cluster. When these ripen they will scatter on the ground, each eventually to create a new plant. Garlic can be harvested when the green shoots have died down, toward the end of the summer. I have never been able to produce a garlic bulb of a size to be found in the market. I don't know why. But the homegrown garlic itself leaves nothing to be desired.

Planting the rest of the garden begins with peas early in April. If they are not in by May twenty-first in this area, they will not produce by July Fourth, when they must be on hand for the traditional dish of creamed new potatoes and peas. Our peas go in early, for they like cool growing weather.

By Memorial Day all garden seeds for the first planting should be in. Early transplants such as tomatoes and peppers must be handled more cautiously, because around here it is possible to have a frost as late as mid-June. Sometimes tenderlings such as these must be protected with frost caps or paper bags on an especially cold night.

All members of the cabbage family can be bought in flats as transplants or they can be sown directly in the garden without, apparently, any delay in maturing. And if they are directly sown, their thinnings are delicious as early cooked greens or as an addition to a salad.

By July we have already frozen spinach, asparagus, and peas. But the real freezing season is in August. The garden has been revving up during July and now it is full-blown. Many varieties of beans are brought into the house and wind up in the freezer in a matter of a couple of hours: bush beans, pole, lima, wax, purple, and more. By late August tomatoes begin to come in. We have already had them green, fried just a little, tart and delicious. The ripe ones stimulate the addicts in the family, of whom I am one. Endless varieties from very small, so delicious, to large. I have discovered how basil combines with ripe tomatoes to produce a flavor I can't resist.

Then comes the corn, also in August, early on if the planting has been early and without frost thereafter. There are many delicious varieties. We have staggered the planting of corn, so as to have it mature through August and into September. If the raccoons are kind to us, we eat it regularly for weeks.

It is said that a corn patch should always be planted uphill from the house. Then one can set a pot of water boiling on the stove, pick the corn, and then *run* back to

59

the kitchen, shuck the corn, and start it cooking without a second's delay. We have also found that corn can be satisfactorily cooked in the oven, in its shucks. This way it cooks in its own juices and loses no flavor in boiling water.

Another vegetable, in a class a bit by itself, is the Jerusalem artichoke. Jerusalem artichokes have nothing to do with Jerusalem, and neither are they artichokes. The plant is like a miniature sunflower, to which it is related, and the roots are the edible part. They are amazingly misshapen, looking a little like gingerroot, and they have a mild flavor and crispy consistency. But they are hard to cook, for they remain solid until suddenly they are mushy. We like them raw, sliced thin, eaten with a bit of cheese as an hors d'oeuvre or as part of a salad.

We raise our own herbs and experiment in their use. They turn out to be quite different from the shelf varieties available in the market. Also, we can use them in their green state, fresh from the garden—an adventure in flavor.

Another great hors d'oeuvre is cucumber, which appears in July as a rule. The long China variety has a firm flesh, small seeds, and lots of juice. They are addictive when served with sour cream mixed with a little fresh dill. I can't get too much of that.

As space appears in the garden in August, we plant for winter: spinach, carrots, and beets. We sow lettuce in the cold frame, where it can be protected from snow during late fall. Once I served fresh lettuce from the cold frame for Christmas dinner, though that was quite a triumph which I only did as a stunt.

Vegetables of the cabbage family may mature during August but often as late as September or even October. Being frost hardy, cauliflower, broccoli, brussel sprouts, kale, and cabbage are good fall vegetables. A light freezing also kills the little worms that often flourish in these plants, a handy dispensation.

By early November the harvest is in, the freezer is full, and one contemplates the coming witner with a sense of satisfaction. The value of this harvest is not only in the food it provides, but also in the psychological satisfaction of growing it.

A main part of any gardening program is maintaining a compost pile, the construction of which has challenged many imaginations. A compost pile can be quite simple, and we have two, one for use as the other matures. Everything from the kitchen except meat scraps and bones (these attract varmints, especially skunks) goes into the pile, unless the pigs and chickens have a higher priority. Scrap paper such as towels and napkins also go into the compost pile.

We have found some rather odd plants coming out of these piles, once they have wintered over and have been spread on the garden. Hybrid varieties of squash have been dumped there, for example, and when their seeds sprout in the spring they do not breed true but come forth in some kind of ancestral form that looks quite odd. Compost also seems to be a good medium for starting fruit pits, for we have gathered several avocado plants and peach trees by this means. But these are short-lived in our climate zone.

The first fruits to appear here are the wild strawberries. By mid-June they can be picked in their favorite haunts—in pastures before they have been grazed, along the edge of woods, on sunny slopes. A neighbor of ours once canned nineteen pints of wild strawberries, and I can only marvel at the time she devoted to picking, hulling, and canning these wonderful delicacies. It is best to pick the whole stem even if only a few berries on it are ripe, because that way the berries remain whole instead of mushing into a sticky mess when you come to hull them. For my part, I have never managed to pick more than a quart or two at a time, and these are quickly gone for shortcake at dinner that night. Small, elusive, and gourmet delicious, wild strawberries are a proper introduction to the fruiting year. Red raspberries and black raspberries, wild or domestic, come along in July. Red raspberries freeze better than any small fruit I know except maybe blueberries. It is impossible to have too many of them, either. Blackberries come at the end of August and are hard to pick because of many strong thorns, but worth the scratches. Bare arms are best for this picking because sleeves catch. But sturdy pants are a must. Blackberry canes seem to reach out to embrace you, but they are more like the spiked iron maiden of medieval times than the more docile raspberries.

Picking wild berries has another aspect that has nothing to do with food for the household. In the days when I was especially hard-pressed, with so much needing to be done right away, or better the day before yesterday, I would grab a small basket and set out for the pasture and woods. I might be away a whole afternoon, roaming where the fancy took me, finding berries here and there in what came to be some of my favorite spots. Some areas of the woods had been opened up by the hurricane of 1938. Berry bushes are the first to return to these open spaces. Then some saplings, which grow into trees, causing the berry bushes to disappear—an interesting round of nature. But I found some good fairly permanent berrying spots: the biggest black raspberries along a certain crumbling stone wall, red raspberries tucked in along a certain hillside under the shoulder of the forest. In the abandoned homestead above our woods, all kinds of interesting things appear, for there are the remains of what was once an extensive orchard. It is now a deer yard, but other things appear from time to time. On my path I once found the dried skull of a small animal and wondered if it was not that of one of our dogs which was last seen chasing a bear and her two cubs. Once there was a porcupine hiding among the bushes that surrounded the old foundation. There were old lilac bushes around what had once been the front door. Here a patch of grass at the base of an old elm, with a long view to the south, where I could stretch out for a while as the pressures drained away, and be at peace with the world. Here I could restore my energies, catch up on my perspective, and be thankful for my blessings. The sounds of the birds and insects, the warmth of the sun, and the blue of the sky refreshed me and made all things seem right. Berries and cream for dessert that night. I recall these interludes with pleasure and gratitude.

In our orchards, summer apples come in August, to be cooked with their skins on. We never spray, so they are safe. Later in the season come the duchess apples, with marvelous flavor. Then the hardier fall apples, good to eat raw and fodder for the cider press. Wild apples make the best cider, worms and all—just a little added protein.

With so much food raised at home, what do we have to buy? Coffee, tea, grains such as rice and oatmeal, flours, citrus fruits, and soap (although I once made this, too). My brothers' nearby gristmill supplies us with the flours. Marshall, having been raised in California, has an abiding passion for artichokes and avocados, so we buy those, too. In late summer we buy a bushel of peaches and freeze them, and also blueberries, for they do not grow in our type of soil. We also buy frozen fish in ten- or twenty-pound lots to store in the freezer. And we buy cheese, Vermont being famous for its cheddar. I have made cottage cheese, but it took more attention than I was willing to give it. Finally, we now buy bread, although for years I made our own. At the end of baking I would put a hot loaf on the bread board with a dish of butter beside it, and in an hour or so it would be gone as members of the household, knowing by the fragrance what was happening, helped themselves. Today, however, a revolution in nutrition has produced many local bakers who know how to produce a good, nutritious loaf, although at a price, and we now are among their devoted customers.

Despite all the changes that have occurred in the past few decades, I can still serve a meal of which every part has been home-produced except the wine.

A Chinese proverb, I am told, says that if you would have happiness for a week, take a wife. If you would have it for a month, kill a pig. And if you would have happiness for a year, plant a garden. I wouldn't know too much about the first. The second is true except that today with cold storage and freezers, the month can be prolonged. But I know for certain that the third proposition is true in every sense.

A garden shows the connection from creation to development to decay to regeneration, in an annual rotation, that is as convincing an argument as any I know for the theory that energy never ends, that it is merely transformed in an unbroken round. Seeds are planted, they grow with the season, develop through stages of maturity, and can be consumed one way or another until the harvest is done. The dead plants decay and are returned to the earth, to be ready to nourish new plantings in the spring.

But food is not the whole of the benefits offered. There is working in the garden, getting your hands into the soil, watching the process of growth, enhancing it with weeding, mulching, TLC, and watering if necessary—to the point where one almost hesitates to eat the little darlings.

And finally there is what can only be called the spiritual benefits of gardening. You have had a rough morning. The children have quarreled, your spouse can't find something needed at once and *where* is it! (More likely, What did you do with it!) Spend the afternoon in the garden and by suppertime everything will be right, including your own peace of mind.

8

Flowers

A FLOWER GARDEN IS JUST ABOUT THE ONLY ASPECT OF LIFE IN the country that has no immediate practical use. Unless you count herbs, which do sometimes qualify as flowers. But if under the label practical you include all kinds of nonmaterial values, then the situation is quite different. In the early days of a new life-style, flowers may hold a low priority in terms of time and attention. But later on they climb the scale until they may even surpass some of the more practical aspects of life in the country.

Traditionally, the care of the flower garden is the responsibility of the woman of the house, and I have known some marvelous examples of such gardens which continue to live in my memory. All of them disappeared soon after they were abandoned by death or divorce. In such places the hardier perennials survive for some years in the sod that surrounds them. Then they too are choked out. In my own garden, to miss a summer season, as twice I have done, is to find a tangled mess of weeds and only a few flowers when I could again turn my attention to it. In these years the garden made its own mulch when I pulled up the weeds and grass and let them lie where they fell.

As good a gardener as a woman can be if she takes an interest in flowers, a man can be even better under the same circumstances. I have observed that if a man takes an interest in household chores, such as cooking, cleaning, and gardening, he is usually better than the average woman. He is also better than the average man. In the garden a man works with the same TLC a woman does, but his imagination seems to be more free, he is often more innovative, and he has more time for the job, not having it as splintered as a woman's time often is among the various household chores that claim her attention, a little here and a little there. No sooner does a woman settle down to a particular job than it is time to feed the baby or prepare a meal.

Creativity is part of flower gardening, but even more of it is called forth when cut flowers are brought into the house to be arranged according to your fantasy. A bowl of flowers on a cold chunk stove in summer is a delight to see, for not only is it lovely to look at but it seems to transform a winter necessity into a summer adventure. It brings the stove right into the summer room, cool and beautiful. In addition, a flower arrangement in an untidy room diverts attention from untidiness, even a mess. Once when Marshall was teaching at a Japanese university, a group of rebel students took over the campus and barricaded themselves in the big administration building. After three months they were ejected, leaving the building knee-deep in litter. The first thing that appeared on the day of liberation was a beautiful flower arrangement on the reception desk in the lobby. A symbol of renewal for the institution.

For an imaginative person, gardening, especially flower gardening, is a relief, a means for soothing the soul, a chance to think of many things besides gardening. It is a chance to observe and make friends with certain plants, and to understand which places in the garden welcome which plants, how certain plants welcome each others' proximity, and which combinations of color complement each other.

The flow of imagination brings satisfaction to the inner mind. One forgets everything but the sight and feel of plants, and the feel of the earth on the hands. For the sake of convention I have several times tried to garden with gloves on, but couldn't stand the resulting frustration. Now I have decided that if someone dislikes the appearance of my hands, he or she should look the other way.

If flower gardens have a lower priority than the vegetable garden, as they usually do, they can be started in a small way. A few plants, perennials for example (a peony, a delphinium, or a violet), can be slipped in here and there wherever there is space. After that, without some strategic planning, some flowers will grow and spread and in time must be controlled. A small clump of Johnny-jump-ups, given to me by a neighbor, in a few years threatened to take over the garden and forced me to be ruthless. These and other self-seeding annuals motivated by an enormous urge to survive, like Shirley poppies and the herb borage, are lovely to look at but deteriorate if they become too crowded; it is necessary to pull the seedlings from the ground by the handfull. Other plants, such as violets and lupines, spread by other means. So does a lovely tiny-blossomed yellow plant which grows in long stems that hug the ground and is known as my lady's bedstraw, because the blossom season produces a fine yellow matting of sweet-smelling flowers, feathery and fine.

We soon adopted a more or less spontaneous plan of growing flowers and vegetables in the same part of the garden. Lettuce, for example, makes a fine border to a path. Beans on poles and sunflowers make a good backdrop on the far margin of the garden. A border of peonies separates the lawn from plantings of vegetables. Red rhubarb chard makes a fine show of color.

In the end, we adopted a policy of allowing every

plant, wild or otherwise, to grow where it wished unless we needed the space for something else. Our garden has become a mishmash that puzzles some onlookers and delights others. We are among the others, partly because we know these wayward friends so well. One year I allowed a thistle to grow and it reached a height of five feet, shaped like the cone of a Christmas tree. The garden must have been extra fertile in that spot because the leaves and spines were a deep, glossy green and the many blossoms were a lively lavender. In the fall these blossoms became fluffy seeds that blew in the breezes. Finally I chopped the plant down, but only to find the following spring that a carpet of tiny prickly thistle plants was growing where the great plant had been. I quickly disposed of the new plants, since a forest of thistles was more than I was prepared to cope with.

So rich is this garden that once a dandelion plant got caught in a clump of phlox and ferns growing some three or four feet high. The dandelion put forth a bloom that traveled, in this thicket, to the surface three feet up, to bloom in the sunlight, I measured the stem of the blossom and marveled at its ingenuity, its tenacity, and its eventual trimuph. The good soil sustained it.

Someone once sent me a small carton of iris rhizomes. These also multiply and if they are separated and replanted now and then, they eventually give you a lot of iris plants— so many in our case that we eventually had a hundred feet or more of border plants, separating garden from lawn. We now enjoy a lovely mass of lavender among the first blossoms of spring.

Then there are the bulbs: daffodils, narcissus, tulips, snowdrops. These bloom early, make a fine show in the garden nourished by their own greenery, and then dis-appear, leaving space for the annuals that bloom in summer and are gone by fall.

Then there are the crocuses that appear on our front

lawn, the first flowers of spring. When they appear we know that winter is almost gone, for they can still show among patches of snow and may even be covered by what is often known as "that white stuff." It is all one to the crocuses. The mail carrier looks for ours each spring, as a kind of signal.

A particularly good place for flowers, especially tall ones like delphinium and hollyhocks, is against a retaining wall. We have a high one that makes a lovely backdrop. There are lilacs and espalier pears here, too, for it faces south and the stones hold the heat of the sun. A lower wall does for hyacinths and other low perennials.

All kinds of gardens are enhanced by shrubs. These offer a change of pace, so to speak, and last for years. Pussy willows grow wild and are also available in some very fancy and lovely domestic varieties. They grow in wet places and long hedge rows, and they are the first shrub to bloom in the spring. Some hardy forsythia are being developed and may eventually survive in Vermont, as they do in many other parts of the country in their natural state and variety. Lilacs and snowballs are traditional around old farmhouses. It is with compassion that one sees these shrubs survive around an old cellar hole. One thinks of the women who planted them and tended them with loving care, often taking the time from soap making or milking or tending the henhouse. Such shrubs must have been islands of delight in an otherwise rugged life.

Another kind of gardening consists of naturalizing wildflowers. A neighbor of ours does not want the responsibility of a garden, so on her many walks in the woods she brings back ferns and other wildflowers and plants them around her house and lawns, mostly in shady places for that is what they are used to. Wildflowers are mostly of the early spring variety if they come from the forest, but buttercups, daisies, and others welcome attention at any time of year. Milkweed, boneset and joe-pye weed will enter wherever you give them an opening. Ferns can be overwhelming; a border of tall ferns hides the foundations of our house in front. They were there when we bought it, and are now more than six feet tall, having thrived on the mulch with which we bank the house every winter.

Another relic of the past that has thrived under our guardianship, is a plot of daylilies behind the woodshed along the path to the study. They are eager growers and we have had to contain them. We planted a patch of flags on the far side of the pond, and a thicket of flowering quince at the foot of the garden. We wound up, I think, by planting all kinds of things as we acquired them, wherever it seemed they would be happy and for the most part we have chosen well—as they soon make known to us.

As summer comes to an end and fall sets in, only a few flowering plants have the hardiness to struggle on until a hard frost finally sends them into hibernation. By that time the householder's attention is turned to houseplants. Some of these have been set for the summer in their pots in shady places in the garden or around the foundations of the house or woodshed, and are now brought in to occupy accustomed places. You look them over, sort them out, discard some, encourage others with a little plant food or desiccated organic fertilizer (another term for dried cow manure), and you are off to a new season.

It was once said that a country kitchen was the best place for houseplants because the steaming kettle on a wood-burning cookstove gave off the right amount of moisture into the air. In some kitchens this is still true. Sunny windowsills or shelves serve the same purpose and make excellent habitats. Some houseplants last for years and become old friends. Moreover, most of them propagate easily in water or wet sand, and it is a constant temptation to allow this kind of multiplication to take place.

If houseplants are your thing—and I must warn you that they can become an obsession—then there are endless varieties to experiment with, to cherish, to talk to, and to listen to. A *New Yorker* cartoon once showed a stout matron à la Helen Hokinson retreating from her window box with a sprinkler can in her hand, her head up, a look of satisfaction on her face. The plants in the window box look at each other and one says, "I thought she'd never shut up."

There are all kinds of rules and procedures for growing plants, in the house and in the garden. Don't be put off by these. Sometimes they are worth following, and many books will tell you how. Sometimes you can do just as well not knowing them. It is a matter of taste and feel on your part. The real rule here, I think, is that whatever gives you pleasure is the right thing to do.

9

Animal Friends

A GOOD CASE CAN BE MADE FOR DISCUSSING ANIMALS AND children together. The two have much in common. Both are active, eager, spontaneous, straightforward, guileless, direct, and affectionate.

Children seem to lose some of these qualities as they grow older and encounter an increasingly artificial environment to which they must adapt or be considered a little odd. Competition with their peers is an important factor in determining behavior and even (eventually) beliefs. Social competition takes on added relevance to the growing child, until the emerging adult is a long way from the simple, honest individual he or she once was.

Our animal friends, on the other hand, lack the intricate thinking mechanisms of humans and remain their original honest and loyal selves to the end. They always behave as children do, and perhaps we relate to them for this reason. We feel a kind of nostalgic remembrance of things past for which we have an occasional yearning amid the many demands on our time and attention that come as we grow older.

In the country, children and their animal friends are pretty much equals and regard themselves as such. When I was a youngster growing up on a farm in Connecticut, my mother had six children and also dogs. So in addition to the children there were usually several dogs of varying ages that formed part of our subculture. Did we play with them or did they play with us? I can't say which of us led the other. The dogs would rush off on their own after some object of great interest, but if we children turned and ran in the other direction, the dogs would turn and rush after us. In any case, Mother recognized the cohesiveness of the group and used the same whistle for all of us when it was time to come in for lunch.

A dog and a child may start out equal in age, but the dog soon becomes mature and thereafter makes itself the protector of the child. This is of special concern in the country where the range of a child's activity is wide. In the case of my own family, a German shepherd bitch called Dain, who came to us when she was only six weeks old and our youngest son, Davis, was two years old, grew with our son for a while and then outstripped him and became his canine nurse-mother, so to speak. Davis was constantly on her mind; he was her charge, her responsibility, and she never left his side when he was outdoors. If she was eating her breakfast when he went out she would interrupt her meal and go with him, perhaps not to return until the end of the morning, when she would clean up her dish.

Once when Davis was three and she (being in heat) was tied up in the woodshed, Dain set up a frantic barking, warning us that our son was running across the lawn toward the pond. On another occasion she warned us that he was using an ax. Again, he was about three. I had got him up from his afternoon nap, let him outdoors, and noting Dain's presence went back to my desk in the living room. I heard Dain trying to let herself into the house by the back door, something she had taught herself and could do quite well. This time she failed, and it caught my attention for this failure was unusual. So I investigated. I found Davis deserted by the dog, using an ax almost as big as he was, trying to split wood. I disengaged the ax just as Dain came running up. In discussing the incident with my husband later, we realized that Dain had been so distraught that she was unable to open the door. Failing this—thus failing to warn me—she had gone up to the woods where Marshall was working to try to get him to come down to the barnyard. But he paid her no attention, supposing only that I had gone to town without her and that she was miffed. In a frenzy she had returned to the barnyard. When she got back and found the ax under control, she lay down, heaving from so much frantic running, and quietly took up her guard again.

In the country the range of animal friends is much wider than in the city where they are usually limited to dogs, cats, and perhaps birds. In the country there are dogs and cats plus kittens and puppies, which almost demand a separate classification. There are also sheep, goats, calves, cows, and possibly hens and roosters. There are pigs of all ages, but especially little ones. It is not for nothing that Piglet has become a famous character in A. A. Milne's delightful stories for children.

Then there are animal friends from the wild, from the woods and fields, although the relationship with these is on a different basis. Some of them can be dangerous. Rabbits, raccoons, woodchucks, even porcupines can be tamed if one is careful and sufficiently tolerant of their tendency to eat the bark off a favorite tree.

A deer may also become a close friend, as a neighbor once proved by rescuing a motherless fawn and bringing it up with his children. It would even ride in the family car. (There are laws against making wild creatures into pets, but in the country it just naturally happens sometimes.) Birds must also be included in this list, especially those that return each year to nest in the same place. These creatures remain in their wild state but often become accustomed to the presence of humans within their domain and establish a certain relationship with them. The mutual response is that of friends.

Cats seem to be in a special class by themselves. Rudyard Kipling was right when he wrote the story about the cat who walked by himself, on his lone way, waving his lone tail. Of all domestic animals, including humans, cats seem to have achieved the ultimate in independence. On a silken cushion in a city drawing room, in the back alley of a city slum, in a barn, or even without shelter, cats seem always on top of the situation.

In the country, some cats prefer to stay in the barn despite warm invitations to join the family in a cozy kitchen. A barn is a pretty free place, with no dogs trying to share the space. There is the daily ration of mouse protein at hand for the catching. If it is a dairy barn, a dish of milk is usually offered in return for helping to control the rodent population. One of our cats which had started as a house cat, preferred the barn and made it her head-quarters, although she was often seen as far as a mile or so away from it. She had her kittens in the barn but would sometimes catch frogs from the pond to feed them as a change from the usual diet of mice.

Without a cat, a country house shows much evidence of invasion from outdoors, because most mice around here come in for shelter in the fall and stay the winter. The mere presence of a cat seems to deter them. Although I am not a cat fancier, I got one in the early days here and have come to admire them for their usefulness as well as for their independence.

However, cats often use up all of their nine lives in a rush—especially a male, if he is not neutered. His courage is often better than his discretion and he usually turns up missing at an early age. Hunters have gotten many of our cats, for some hunters will shoot at anything that moves, especially at the end of a frustrating day and if the gun is still loaded. We have found some pathetic little carcasses. In addition, a fox may be hungry, or a dog may have a grudge.

Nevertheless, we have found that in the house, the reigning cat is boss of other cats and also of dogs. I have seen one small cat chase a German shepherd around the kitchen because of some fancied threat to her litter behind the stove. Outdoors it is a different matter. Seemingly by mutual understanding, a cat is fair game for a dog. It may be all in fun, but outdoors a cat keeps an eye on a dog and takes its precautions. A high beam in the shed or a branch in a tree is often a handy refuge from the not-always-so-playful barking of a dog freed from the confines of house discipline.

A real hazard to young animals, especially kittens and puppies, is how children handle them. A young child does not know what hurt means unless the child actually experiences it, and he or she must learn that animal friends can also be hurt. It is a lesson that can be quickly learned and understood. We have a cat now that must have been mishandled by a child when it was a kitten because she cannot stand to be picked up around the middle or fondled around the head and forequarters. She is affectionate and responsive to petting, but only from the waist down. She came to us as a stray, having no doubt been abandoned by her summer owners when they returned home in the fall. She was thin, starving, and exhausted when she came into our woodshed and Marshall fed her. She would not come into the house for three days. Then she accepted Marshall's invitation and came in tentatively. He christened her Violette.

Violette spent the first few weeks gaining weight and restoring her strength. She ate, slept, ate again, and went back to sleep on a cushion in a rocking chair. During that period she would always sleep in the same chair, and it is interesting to note that she has not had anything to do with that chair since then. She was quiet, courteous, friendly, considerate, and clean—so much so that our idea of her character was slightly off center. But this was soon remedied when she reached her normal stage of development, as soon as her biological clock, so to speak, was back on time. For then she also became a hoyden, a tomboy, playing vigorously with all kinds of makeshift toys, running around the house, and becoming quite demanding in her ways.

We think Violette must have been brought up with a dog because she has doggy habits, like lying in front of the chunk stove much as a dog will lie on the hearth rug, and sometimes picking up a small stick in the woodshed and walking around with it in her jaws. She often sits on top of a cupboard where through a small window she has a view of the walk to the shed. Our son waves to her as he comes along on his way to the house, and she jumps to the floor to greet him as he enters the house. She also seems to be a man's cat because she favors my husband and our son, instead of me, who feeds her.

In the barn, a calf is an attractive pet but by the time it has become a cow it has lost its appeal. Chicks that grow into hens still respond to humans if the humans can still respond to their rather specialized qualities. Marshall can and does. Young sheep and goats often respond readily to humans who take an interest in them. Pigs make wonderful pets at all ages but especially when young, for they are intelligent and playful. Marshall can lean on the stone wall of their pen and watch them for long periods of time. And when they are older—and about ready for the freezer—they will rub against his legs when he goes into their enclosure.

But the ultimate pet for children in the country is a pony, for here is the means of leaving home base and exploring along back roads and in the fields and woods. A pony becomes useful to a child when the child reaches the age of five or so, and remains reliable until the child's legs begin to hang too close to the ground (perhaps around ten or so). A pony, or a horse for that matter, must be managed more than most pets. Despite the big dark eyes that look so intelligent, a pony is not very smart. It can be trained, but only with a lot of time and patience. Perky ears, arched neck, a flowing mane and tail describe a magnificent creature whose brain, alas, is small. I suppose they have too much imagination, because they tend not to see things as they are. An unfamiliar object or noise becomes a spook, a tiger in the bushes. The response is irrational. Instead of defending itself, a pony will shy and run. A hangover from the primeval, no doubt, but disconcerting to a rider. For this reason, a pony in harness wears blinders on its eyes.

Ponies and horses can and do teach manners. A swift kick with a hind leg or (even more damaging) with a foreleg striking out in front, tells one where to stand, and not to be lost in a moment of abstraction. A nip on the arm or a sudden right angle turn, which can throw an unwary rider, proves a lesson. A favorite trick in the woods is to pass beneath a low branch of a tree, scraping the rider onto the ground. You might say that the pony has the upper hoof in these cases. Once when it happened to me, I distinctly saw a snicker on the lips of my mount as I got up and climbed back into the saddle.

Small children are said to make pets out of all kinds of uncouth creatures such as frogs, snakes, beetles, and mice. These sometimes even inhabit a cozy pocket, much to mother's distress if she comes on them unexpectedly. A tolerant mother will remember her own childhood, when she may have welcomed equally strange creatures—if she has had the good fortune of being brought up in the country.

In the nature of things children grow up and leave home, and animal friends take on an even greater importance in the home than they did before. They offer loyal and affectionate companionship. They never judge, they always respond to one's mood, and they are always there but not obtrusive. They laugh when you do and weep when you do, too, although not with tears. They will play if that is your need of the moment, and they will watch, going outside with you or lying quietly at your feet when you are inside. I am describing dogs, of course, but cats also respond to your mood and will even go for a walk with you if so inclined. A quiet cat curled up on your lap is a comforting thing.

It is a sad day when an animal friend reaches the end of its tether (so to speak). Cats usually manage their own demise when they run out of lives. But a cat that spends most of its time in the house may reach an advanced age, and in a country environment staying inside is about the only way that end is achieved. Both dogs and cats may live longer than is comfortable for them. I have wept more tears over the death of a dog, deliberate though it may have been, than over most other circumstances.

When pets are treated as human beings they respond as human beings. They even talk, if a human's ear is attuned to that kind of language. A certain dog I once knew was said by her owner to be able to talk all right but to have had a little trouble articulating.

Not for her owner, she didn't. He could read her mind and was usually able to respond to a request. A look, a sound, a thump of the tail, a smile, a snort, a rub on the shins, a certain kind of cry for hunger and another for wanting out—there are many kinds of animal language.

The low, welcoming whinny of a pony, for example, is understood by an alert human. And a dog often seems to know what is in the mind of its human companion, even when no words are spoken.

In addition to companionship, a dog is useful as watcher and guardian. In the country such an animal is handy to have around. I don't mean a guard dog that would attack an intruder, although these days that also might be an asset. I mean the kind that is always on the alert when someone is coming on the place whom the dog does not know. Such a dog will tell you about it with a certain kind of bark that you quickly recognize. It will say, "Here is a stranger. Come and check it out." Often an intruder with malicious intent will go on by, because a dog looks pretty fierce—as some do, with teeth showing, lips drawn back, and the hair on the back standing up. If the dog has a broad head, the illusion is all the greater. Our present dog can put on quite a show but has never been known to sink a tooth into any living thing. Even in a peace-loving dog a bark can be made to sound authoritative to a stranger. Today our dog will greet a stranger and follow him or her to our door, barking the while to alert us and then retreating when one of us shows up to take charge.

In the country, two dogs are harder to handle than one, for they love to run in company in the woods and may run a deer. This is illegal, and in Vermont the game warden who sees them has the right to shoot them on the spot. Usually the warden merely warns the owner on the first offense, but after that the warden will be on the alert.

We have had three bird dogs that didn't take much interest in deer and we have had not trouble of that kind. The first, Chip, found it a little hard to get used to his freedom after having lived in a kennel to the age of five. He regularly took advantage of it twice a day running in the woods, apparently just to remind himself of how good it felt. He really concentrated on it. Once he passed me on a woodland path and didn't even turn his head when I called to him.

Chip's son, Ravi, had a little broader outlook, having been brought up in a state of freedom from the outset. But he had his limits. Each day he made the rounds of a number of woodchuck holes on the place. One was in a hedge near the pond. He seemed to have a particular dislike for its inhabitant because he would harass it. One evening as we were enjoying a cookout by the pond he harried it more than usual. He took the woodchuck by the scruff of the neck and shook the life out of it, the standard method. We called to him but he picked up the carcass and ran off in the opposite direction as if to say, "This is my business; you stay out of it." Sometime later he joined us at the cookout, coming from the opposite direction from down behind the barn, where presumably he had buried his catch. I don't think he ever killed another woodchuck, or anything else for that matter. Nor did he go back to this carcass, for if he had we would have known it by the unmistakable smell.

The affection shown by a dog is invariably honest. Not so with cats, for often enough there is an element of calculation in it. When they brush against you, for example, they seem to be saying they can't live without you. But after years of being deceived I now know that it merely means they are hungry and will you please oblige. When they curl up on your lap often enough it means that they like the warmth it provides. Sometimes their affection seems only incidental.

But cats do show real affection, too, and other human qualities. They may also have a strong sense of possession. I once had a small, black long-haired female named

Mumtaz Mahal after the woman for whom the Taj Mahal was built. The woman was Persian and we thought the cat might be somewhat Persian. At the time we also had a large neutered tabby called Eldridge. One day I was sitting on the couch with Eldridge on my lap. He was one of those really affectionate animals. Mumtaz was sleeping, curled up in my sewing basket on the table beside me. She woke up and noticed Eldridge on my lap. She rose up to her full minuscule height with arched back and hair standing up, and *screamed* at him. It was an astonishing sound seemingly from deep in the wild. Eldridge, who was a mite slow-witted, took the situation in consideration for a moment and then got up, moved off my lap, and resettled himself beside me. This satisfied Mumtaz, who curled up in her basket again and went back to sleep. Both Eldridge and I had gotten her meaning. However, Eldridge was not as amused as I was.

Having lost my sight before she came to us, I have never seen Violette, our present cat, although I do know what she looks like: mostly white with a calico tail and a few calico markings around the head. She and I have a close understanding. She tells me when she wants food or when she wants to be let out to the shed, and I know the signals. When she is ill, I know it, too. I know when she needs clean water in her bowl. I listen to the tones in her voice. If she fails to greet me in the morning as I am getting coffee cups off a certain shelf, I know that she is either mad at me or is not in the house. She doesn't like to lie on my lap when I am knitting, so if she decides to favor me, I put my knitting down. She is a cat of long memory and not much imagination, whereas Mumtaz had a long memory plus imagination and the ability to alter an old habit when she considered it useful.

For example, when Mumtaz came to us from a rather posh family in Washington, she would eat nothing unless it came from a can. Then when Eldridge joined us she met the competition by eating everything he ate, including grain. In the end she did without the canned stuff. She would stake out her place of repose for several days at a time: now in this chair, now on the couch. Then for no good reason we could see, she would change to something else. One of her favorite sites was on the chair to Marshall's desk. She stayed longest there and came back to it more often, despite the constant danger of being sat on by an absent-minded professor. Or because of it. She seemed to like challenge.

Animals seem to know when their time has come. A cat will sometimes find a dark corner in a shed or in an attic in which to curl up until the life has gone out of it. Dogs also tend to hide when the end is near, even more so than cats, because they seem to need solitude, away from those they love. Often, when the end is coming, both cats and dogs seem to know it before we do. When Mumtaz was old and became ill, I let it go until it seemed she was in pain. Then one day I wrapped her in a towel and held her on my lap as Marshall drove us to the veterinarian. She lay quietly with her head in the palm of my hand. At the veterinarian's we waited for half an hour. The waiting room was confused with people and other animal patients but Mumtaz took no notice. Then the veterinarian came, asked a question or so, and then gently took her away. And I lost a friend.

When it came to be Chip's time to go I put it off as long as I could—too long. He was old, deaf, and ailing, and he had arthritis. One morning he sat in the middle of the kitchen, his front legs spread at awkward angles, and looked at me. As plainly as he could he was asking, "How much longer does this have to go on?" I went right to the phone and called the veterinarian. Marshall carried him to the car, wrapped up in a blanket. Chip loved that car and lay quietly, almost philosophically, I am tempted to think. The veterinarian carried Chip into the surgery. I went with him and stayed with him until the lethal injection had done its work. The veterinarian pulled the blanket back around him and carried him back to the car. Then I brought him home, in tears as I drove. We buried him near the pond and I later planted a bed of Japanese irises to commemorate the spot. Chip was an old and dear friend and I think of him often. So human was he that once when I took him with me on a visit to my brother, and I remarked that I thought Chip would be a man in the next incarnation, my brother's reply was, "Hell, he was a man in the last one."

There does in fact seem to be a very fine line of demarcation between animals and humans: between all kinds of animals and all kinds of humans, for the variety in one group seems to be as great as in the other. The difference may be more marked in the city than in the country, where a wider base in nature provides all creatures with a natural habitat. And by all creatures I mean people, too. In the country, people and their animal companions begin at the same point and they develop, sometimes together, according to their own needs and talents. Their life spans are different, to be sure, but who can say that one achieves less than the other, or more. Nor does it matter. In the country achieving is of less importance than simply living and enjoying and being true to oneself, for animals and humans alike.

10

Sex

IN THE COUNTRY THERE IS A CONSTANT ROUND OF LIFE AND death. And so it is in the city, too, but much less evidently so except in the case of humans. In the city a few insects and birds, and stray cats and dogs, and human beings are about the only living things one notices. But in the country one is surrounded by living things that eventually die— living things of the animal kingdom, that is. The vegetable kingdom is another story, albeit a similar one of birth, development, decay, and re-creation.

In the country one finds the traditional sexual symbols: the birds and the bees. Among birds the first sign that mating has occurred comes with the subsequent building of a nest. The creative schedule is on course. With bees the mating is equally out of sight, taking place in flight, high in the air. In the course of it, the queen bee is fertilized for life, while the drone loses his life instantly.

The woods and fields are full of small animals mating at the proper time, raising their young, helping them to develop, and then leaving them to their own devices to start the round all over again. It is a round punctuated by death, decay, and return to the good earth to provide fertilizer for whatever member of the animal or vegetable kingdom that happens to be nearby. Rabbits, squirrels, beavers, opossums, wildcats, woodchucks, foxes, deer, field mice, moles, bears, and porcupines copulate, populate, develop, and die. (A question often asked in Vermont is, "How do porcupines make love?" To which the response is, "*Very* carefully."

Among domestic animals, dogs and cats are far from discreet in their love affairs. Although cats are capable of some discretion, one always knows when the urge is there. Dogs have no shame at all, and a male will often travel long distances to find a female whose scent he has picked up. He will stay around her for several days seeking to seduce her and then find his way home, bedraggled, hungry, sore-footed, and exhausted. Even bloody, for chances are he has had to fight several other dogs for the privilege he may or may not have secured.

We once had a fine white and black ticked English setter of the small Llewellyn variety. My psychiatrist sister was petting him one day and commented, "Chip's trouble is he doesn't know he's a man." In consequence we bought him a wife, still not quite grown, so he could bring her up to suit his whims. In due course estrus occurred, but she was still too young to be bred, so we kept her and Chip away from each other. But Chip knew that she would welcome his attentions if only we would let them alone, and he led a frustrated life for a few days. Next time around, however, there were no frustrations, and Chip's personality took a marked change toward manhood. And when the pups were born, at first he was incredulous, and then became a bully.

Another of our dogs, one of Chip's sons, grew to "doghood" without having experienced sex. We would hitch him to a doghouse in the woodshed at night, and one morning I opened the back door and found him all tied up on a very beautiful white hound dog. I carefully closed the door until the tie had broken and she had gone on about her business. But thereafter Ravi was a different dog, and even challenged Chip one evening when our daughter brought her little female dog into the kitchen. Son had father on his back on the floor when we separated them. Chip got up, shook himself, and looked at his son as though to say, "For Heaven's sake, what got into you?"

Nowadays, both cats and dogs are often "fixed," as the saying is around here, when progeny are not welcome. Even so, the cats have a hard time staying out of trouble. A cat has many enemies and needs all of its nine lives to make it to a natural death. Only a nonbelligerent female who spends most of her time in the house has much chance of a long life. Unneutered males need more than nine lives, for like unneutered dogs they too travel for miles if they become aware of a female in heat. A tomcat may be absent from home for several weeks at a time, and not all of it in attendance of one female. Tomcats roam the neighborhood, especially at night. Indeed, if a man in Vermont lives so far from civilization that his neighbors rarely see him, he is said to live so far back he has to keep his own tomcat.

Other domestic animals, such as cows, horses, goats, and sheep have sex according to the convenience of their owner instead of at the sole dictates of nature. A stallion is seldom seen on a Vermont farm unless it is a horse breeding farm; it can be a rambunctious animal and must be handled with care. Bulls are also seldom seen, because the science of artificial insemination has been advanced to the point where a farmer can select the sire he wants from a semen bank, and a technician does the job with tubes and syringes. This eliminates the need for keeping a difficult animal to handle on the farm. In the old days a barnyard would often contain a special breeding rack in which a heifer could be hitched while the bull, with most of his weight on the rack, did his job. Occasionally one saw a bull in a pasture with a herd of heifers, which at the end of the season would be labeled as pasture-bred to mean that the exact date of conception was unknown. The presence of a bull under these circumstances was also a sign to keep out of that pasture.

Sheep and goats don't seem to present much of a problem. They come into estrus at a certain time of year, are duly bred, and produce on schedule. Births, though, are sometimes complicated, and the farmer must sometimes stay up all night to help a struggling ewe.

Pigs present a problem, because unless one keeps a boar, a nasty animal with long tusks and uncertain temper, the sow must be taken to its mate. The question is, which is the right day? Signs of estrus are not always definite. One way to tell, we hear, is to throw one's leg over the back of the sow. If she humps a bit, she's ready. Another Vermont story tells of a man who had no way to transport his sow to his neighbor's boar except in a wheelbarrow. He loaded her onto the wheelbarrow on what he thought was the right day and wheeled her to his neighbor's boar, but nothing happened. The next day brought the same result. But when the man went to the pig yard on the third day, he found the sow sitting in the wheelbarrow.

And chickens. A hen doesn't need a rooster around to produce eggs, only to produce fertile eggs. Here the main problem is finding a rooster that isn't too big for the hens. We did that once. We had a flock of laying hens, rather small ones, and we also had a flock of meat birds that grew very large indeed. We selected a likely looking rooster of the meat breed and let him in with the hens. He was so masterful we called him Hercules, but he was too hard on the hens and ended up on our dining table.

And what, finally, of humans? Shall we draw a discreet line here? By no means. One has only to mention how warm a bed can be on a cold night, with the mercury down below zero and the bedroom on the cool side, too, contrasted to a bedroom in the city, surrounded by sound and intrusive lights. The city bedroom may be richly decorated, with heavy drapes, but can you ever fully exclude sound? Then consider a country bedroom with no shades and just token drapes, with only the sky and the stars visible. A few sounds in the morning, to be sure, as when the birds wake up and begin their day. I once heard a bird start his morning song a bit off key, it seemed. Then he cleared his throat and started again, this time a clear note, and he went about his business.

Nor, in the country are humans confined to the bedroom. For there is all of outdoors. I do not suggest rolling around in snowdrifts, but consider a bright, warm day from May to late in an Indian summer, say October: a side hill among the pines overlooking a stream, or deep in the forest. A fallen log on a mossy bank provides privacy, although none is really needed. Or a grassy ledge, a small, grassy clearing with a wide view of forest, pastures, and meadows. In a pasture under a white birch, its branches reaching high toward a bright blue sky. There are times when the house is full of family, that love on location is not only more private but also more satisfying from both the physical and the aesthetic points of view.

I do not wish to increase the world's already over-populated state, but I do recommend the adventure of love under a big sky or on the mosses of a woodsy glen.

11

Children

IN THE CITY THE SOLES OF CHILDREN'S SNEAKERS WEAR OUT before the uppers do, and in the country it is the uppers that give out first. In the city a child runs, walks, and plays on hard pavement, on sidewalks, streets, promenades, school grounds and public playgrounds. All are paved and cause the soles of all footwear to take a beating. In the country, on the other hand, a child plays, roams, and runs on soft surfaces: on meadows and pastures, on the forest floor, and on dirt roads. He or she climbs trees, scrambles over rocks, mucks about in barns and haylofts, explores woodsheds, moves through thickets, climbs over old logs and fallen frees. A country child also rolls in the grass, tussles with companions, wades through ponds and brooks, climbs into silos and up and down ladders. And the uppers of his or her sneakers show it.

When we lived in Brooklyn Heights for a while I observed children trying to play ball on a quiet residential street. I saw them running along the promenade and playing in the public playgrounds. They seemed happy enough, but I regarded them as badly handicapped with no woodshed to play in and to explore. For a child's imagination flourishes in a woodshed. Albert Einstein is said once to have remarked that imagination is better than knowledge, and he should know. The treasures of a woodshed with its firewood and tools, its odd collections of things that might come in handy should some special occasion arise (and must be saved on that account, although it is more likely that they will never be used), challenge a child's imagination and ingenuity in ways that no city child can experience.

A country childhood creates the framework for the future development of personality and character, a framework that subtly stresses creativity, patience, and the adventure of finding a way to do something new and different. This framework matures with the individual and helps him or her in the future. Here is created an almost unconscious understanding of the interrelationships among people and ideas, and among plants, animals, and the seasons. There is formed a matrix that becomes increasingly useful in later years. The seasons, for example, come to mean something more than dirty snow on a city street or a few struggling green leaves on a sparse tree (on the trees in a park, if one is lucky enough to live near one). In the country, life is all of a piece, and the child, like a sponge, soaks up impressions which in later life form the basis for many understandings that in the city are largely lacking because much of nature—except the human—is missing.

In addition, the country creates the conditions that a child needs until he or she reaches the age of at least twelve. The family may move around in pursuance of careers, in this country or abroad, but if there is always home ground to return to the sense of belonging is not lost. Home is not where you hang you hat—if you even wear one—but where you store your luggage, hang your baskets, and collect your treasures, bringing them out when you need to and putting them away when you don't.

Places away from home have their advantages and

become part of one's being just as the contents of a woodshed do. These places have their special joys to be experienced and delighted in, and to do without them would be to limit one's life. But having experienced them, it is good to go home again. Contrary to Thomas Wolfe, you can do this—even to a childhood home, as your children have proved.

Moreover, having experienced the adventure of living away from home for a time, it is also good to go home again in order to consider these adventures from a perspective that adds to their value. Children can participate in this exercise, which helps in developing their personalities, character, talents, perceptions, and sensitivities. At the same time it enhances the security that home provides.

The French word *souche* seems to describe this function of the home in the country, better than any word I know in the English language. Literally, souche is the stump from a tree that has been cut down and then grows sprouts that become saplings and finally trees. By extension, it describes the home base, village, town, or community from which a person or the person's parents have sprung. It is the place of origin of a family. In Switzerland one's souche may be two or three generations in the past, but it remains the souche of the individual, who has a loyalty to it no matter where he or she may have strayed.

Our youngest son traveled with us for almost ten years beginning at age four, to California, Puerto Rico, Florida, Turkey, England, New York (Brooklyn), and Minnesota. He attended school in each of these places as well as in Vermont, sometimes for several months or a whole semester at a time. After college and five years in a large western city, he is now home again, determined to stay here for the rest of his life. A visitor once asked me if any of our children were sufficiently interested in this place to carry it on once we have stepped out, and I told her with some amusement that yes, our youngest son insisted on it. It was a moment of shared pleasure that I could assure her on this point.

In a child's country life the woodshed is probably basic to every other aspect of the home, with the possible exception of the kitchen and the woman or man who occupies it.

If a workbench is part of the shed, and usually it is, the variety of tools, which is another word for toys, is infinite. First there is the wood itself and the tools to handle it. Saws, axes, mauls, cant hooks, and, under strict supervision, chain saws. And, when it is still used, the crosscut saw is a challenge. Accompanying these items are the tools that maintain and sharpen them, a separate classification in themselves, and it is a matter of self-mortification to get them mixed in with more ordinary tools.

A chain saw must be used or supervised by one who knows how to handle it, for to misuse it can be lethal. To learn to use an ax is to learn how to split a piece of wood, which can become a fine art in determining grain and how to take advantage of it. A hatchet soon leads to the pleasure of splitting kindling wood without taking the fingers off.

Piling firewood in the shed is another fine art some people instinctively understand, while others with a less sure sense of balance and order never master it. Or they at least learn the hard way, with tumbled piles to frustrate and possibly to teach them the rules. Wood is piled according to classification: longer pieces for the fireplace, heavy chunks for the chunk stoves, and smaller, shorter pieces for the cookstove. To one with a fine sense of balance, piling wood is a delightful source of recreation plus exercise that is its own reward.

At the workbench itself, or hanging on a nearby wall,

are the carpentry tools. Even if not often used, their appearance conveys a knowledge of what they are for. Hammers, screwdrivers, saws, as well as nails, screws, dowels, bolts, nuts, and spikes of many different sizes. Pliers and many different wrenches, files, and rasps to use for various purposes. Saws and ripsaws to try to tell apart. Nail pullers, squares, miter boxes, wrecking bars, and pinch bars. Plus a host of miscellany, like brads, chisels, planes, levels, and a myriad of unrelated bits and pieces such as leather scraps, the remains of harnesses, brass rings, water pipe, and countless washers, tapes, braces, tapes, sandpaper, and steel wool. Then there are the power tools, like drills and polishers. The accumulation grows with the family, a great hoard of things that might come in handy some day, or might never. But you can't really tell, so don't throw them out. Ever.

Then there are varnishes, shellacs, polishes, glues, paint brushes and the means of cleaning them, oils and oil cans, fine pieces of finished wood, shims, broom handles, bits of metal sheeting, twine, wire, and cable. All of these have had, and still may have, their uses. An adult may be hard put to say just what, but a child will have no trouble at all, so much fresher and more fertile is a child's brain, ingenuity, and inventiveness.

In addition to these challenges to the imagination are the garden tools; however, these may be limited as toys because to use them generally means work. Anyhow, it is work only for those who do not have an innate feel for the soil and hence for gardening. This sometimes comes at a later time in life, because it seems to take an extra step in thought to go from the use of a hoe to the growing plant to the harvest. It is the exceptional child who can see ahead this far and get a kick out of the initial use of a garden tool.

The list of garden tools is large: hoes, rakes, shovels,

and spades of many kinds, trowels, weeders, cultivators, potato hooks, even pitchforks now that mulch gardening is so popular.

Because gardening is now more popular than ever, the gardening fraternity has expended itself in the invention of a host of easy-to-use mechanical tools. But there is some question in my mind whether these are not more costly and less satisfying to the soil in their use. For large commercial gardening there is no question about it, but for the home gardener I wonder if the need isn't self-induced—well illustrated when one of our neighbors once had his grandson visiting him for the summer vacation. The boy was fourteen at the time, and the juices were beginning to flow to the point where he was taking a keen interest in the girls in the neighborhood. One day the grandfather stopped in our yard and said he had sent his grandson home. "Why did you do that?" asked my husband. "Hurmph," said the grandfather, "soon as they can, they think they must." And so it is with advanced, expensive garden tools. As soon as they are available, gullible homesteaders think they must use them. We have found most of them, indeed all of them, to be more trouble than they are worth. The only piece of garden machinery (if you can call it that) on our place is a garden cart, which is altogether useful and seldom needs maintenance. Though we do have a snowblower and two lawnmowers, the first can be dispensed with, but the latter have made themselves indispensable—simply because their presence inspired their use.

In a country home the barn is another source of infinite delight—inventiveness in playing games, and resourcefulness in devising adventure. It is a prime source of education for any child exposed to its infinite offerings. Preferably it should be an old barn that has accumulated generations of "oddments and endments," so to speak:

old tools, bits and pieces of machinery, a horse blanket in tatters, obsolete harnesses, calf pens, buckets, nests of mice in the hay, a resident cat or two (very much alive), ropes, ladders to secret places, mounds of hay to be burrowed in or tunneled in, places to hide, perhaps a silo to climb into, cow's stanchions, and horse stalls. In the mind of a child, each suggests a use that may be quite different from the original intent. To him or her, every item has its unique worth. Scrap lumber, bits of tin, a horse whip found in some unlikely corner. In our barn we once found a hidden diary nearly a century old, and up among some rafters, a woman's blouse, blue and white checked, with pretty buttons.

But a barn has its practical uses, too, if your home is a subsistence farm. Modern barns are small because the number of animals is usually limited. Draft horses are no longer useful in farming, and hay is bailed and fits into much less storage space than loose hay. But our barn is very old and serves every purpose for which barns were once built. More than half of it is for the storage of hay, and in addition it includes a horse stable, carriage shed, cow stable, heifer line, maternity pen, bull pen, chicken coop, harness room, and a drying floor under the gable meant no doubt for beans or corn. In the basement is a large storage area for manure, which when kept under cover keeps all of its original nutrients instead of having them drain away with the rains. To all of this we added a silo.

Then there are the animals that inhabit these premises. We have had them all at one time or another, and have refashioned and remodeled their quarters as needed. Once we had an enormous Yorkshire sow in the horse barn, and she farrowed in the box stall meant for horses. But we had no horse at the time. That part of the barn is now an athletic club and a cider mill. Another area has been converted into a storage unit for surplus furniture. The cow stable is no longer occupied by cows since ours now live on our partner's farm. But the barn is tight and well-maintained and could be put to all of its original uses if needed.

A country childhood does more than develop imagination and ingenuity, of course. There are also practical matters. At age six or seven a child can learn how to enter a horse's stall, back the horse out, and lead it to water. Then the child cleans the stall, puts the horse back in and feeds it hay, grain, or both. Such a child learns quickly how to avoid being stepped on, how to avoid hind legs and forelegs, how to groom, and how to harness. He or she can also learn how to pick up a horse's hooves to inspect for stones caught in the frog, or for loose shoes, how to cool a horse off after hard work, and how to bed it down for the night.

Then there is the care of the harness, which must be cleaned and mended or replaced. This is most delightfully done on a rainy day when the coziness of the stable contrasts with the falling rain. Indeed, the horse stable becomes a workshop in the education of a child, as does the rest of the barn.

Cows are less companionable than horses and ponies, but young calves can be playmates. Except that a calf will not substitute for a pony, as I once discovered when I tried to ride one. I was a sturdy child and a calf does not have much strength. We landed in a heap of legs against a wire fence, and the calf was more shaken than I.

On a modern farm the work team of horses has been replaced by tractors of all kinds and sizes, and among our neighbors, some boys as young as eight or nine can handle them with skill and a huge delight once they have learned to recognize the dangers. And it is not too long before they can take a rig to the fields for plowing or harrowing. If there is any mechanical ability in a child, it is soon developed in the use of such machinery. From tractor to car is a simple step, so be warned.

The degree to which a child in the country becomes a part of his or her environment is illustrated by a few examples that I have observed. The farm son of a farmer partner fell off a hay wagon in the field, landed on his hands, and broke his wrist when he was about eight years old. He wore a cast and had his arm in a sling for several weeks. But that turned out to be an asset in at least one instance: The children decided to move a campsite from one field to another, which meant transporting a number of bricks for the fire hole some distance. The boy with the sling could carry more than his mates by simply filling the sling as one would fill a bag.

Cows need salt, and a big square chunk was usually kept on a stick in the pasture for the cows to lick as they wanted. While roaming the pastures, the children would commonly pass by the salt and give the cake a lick themselves. It was pretty good, said our youngest in alluding to it. Then at lunch one day he looked out toward the lower pasture on the other side of the pond and said, "You know what the cows do down at the gate?" "Yes I do," I replied. And then with some apprehension, "What about it?" "It tastes," he said, "like frambled eggs." Well, I thought, too late to do anything about it now.

In the country a child's education begins as soon as he or she can crawl, but eventually that child must also go to school. Education is usually a local concern, controlled by a locally elected school board and paid for through local taxes with some help from the state. Some local school systems are very good indeed, and in these cases it will usually be found that local citizens take an active interest in the matter. Others could stand some improvement. A school system is as good as the community wants it to be and is willing to work to make it that way. Quality depends on the quality of the individual teachers and the caliber of the school board. Drugs and alcohol are a problem in small towns today, as they are elsewhere, and must be dealt with skillfully. Schools in the country are smaller than in the city or the suburbs, though, and the problem is more manageable. Again, it is likely to be the concern of the community that is controlling. A feeling of security in the home at a time when the child is trying to become independent helps here as it helps in the city.

As the child becomes increasingly independent, he or she soon learns adult ways of behavior, social artifices, indirection, and competition with peers, especially socially. The need to comply with peer pressure is inescapable. The anguish that accompanies these developments may be mitigated to some extent by the presence of a haven in the home. Such a haven may not be just what the young person wishes to acknowledge, of course. In fact, he or she may make it plain that home is not on his or her agenda, now or ever. But it is, all the same, and in some corner of his or her being the young person recognizes it and is grateful, though there are times when it would be impossible for him or her to admit it. A haven is a haven is a haven, constituting a rock of stability in a young person's background to which to turn with relief when the occasion warrants.

The time just prior to when a young person is legally free to drive a car is probably one of the hardest for a parent to cope with. By then the young person has become involved in school athletics, especially basketball which is a winter diversion in a small town. There is much nighttime travel to neighboring towns for games. If the family lives in the country, this creates a driving job for someone to take the resident ball player to the bus and then to meet and return the player to his or her bed. Hours tend to be late.

Nor is the situation much better when the legal driving age has been reached, for now the young person is on his or her own, at the wheel of a car. It is a hard time for parents, and they need all the strength of their home environment, plus faith in their children, to cope with it.

After school comes college for many, and then a job, marriage, and their own home and family. But in Vermont there has been a long tradition for sons, and sometimes married daughters, to remain on the farm with the family business, maintaining it and caring for aging parents as well. In modern times this tradition has evolved in a slightly different way. Young people now sometimes try the outside world for a period of years and then return to the home place to carry on from there; or they have their own place nearby, from which they can supervise the home place until it is their time to take over; or they have their own nearby home but work at some job in town or within commuting distance.

With several children doing this, a family compound is created, each member working with the others as needed. There are three examples of this arrangement around us, only one of which is a farm. Ours is a subsistence farm, shared to some degree by our daughter and her husband, who live a quarter mile away, and to a full degree by our youngest son and his companion, who live in a cottage within a stone's throw from the main house. Included also are our daughter's stepson and his family. Among the four households we cover a wide range of activities and capabilities. We sometimes pool transportation and lend assistance in many areas from land and forest management to syrup making, beekeeping, plumbing, and carpentry.

When Marshall and I bought this place it never occurred to us to plan for our retirement in any detail. We would, we took for granted, remain here on the place. We did not suppose that any of our children would be around to care for us in the doddering stage. But our youngest son has returned here with his companion and has gradually slipped into the role of caretaker of the place, if not yet of us, although his sense of responsibility seems already to include that aspect of the matter. He and she do many things for us without being asked, and we do things for them as well. We also do many things jointly, such as gardening and caring for the land and the forests. All of this happened a little by accident, but the result is a good feeling. By working together and by supplementing each other's efforts, we have the best garden in the county, and the most handsome grounds and nicest looking home in this part of the township. We didn't plan it that way, but by following a rural way of life as a gradual process dictated by simple country living, that is the way it has happened.

12

Energy

IN THE COUNTRY THERE ARE TWO MAIN KINDS OF ENERGY AND they interlock at several points. The first is material—mainly fuels—and includes electricity, oil, gasoline, and wood. The second is generated by the body, both human and animal, if animals are used for work. The two kinds of energy come together, especially in the supplying and the using of wood.

The most expensive part of living in the country is the cost of fuel, and fortunately it is here also that many critical savings may be made. Oil, gasoline, and especially electricity with all the various uses to which it may be put in the form of appliances can be costly. It pays to be able to reduce these requirements, and fortunately it can be done.

Appliances can especially be reduced to a minimum, indeed to the barest minimum, for advantages at both ends: their cost on one hand, and a satisfying way of doing things on the other. An electric mixer is a great thing to have in the kitchen, but an old-fashioned eggbeater is easier to use, clean, and store. The skeptic has only to give it a try.

On a larger scale we proved the possibility of the non-appliance life-style by living here for several years without electricity and without central heating. Now after forty-three years we still have no central heating and have never paid a cent for fuel oil. Nor have we ever been cold. Nor has the cellar ever frozen. So I can say with some confidence that people ordinarily do not need all the conveniences they think they need, or all they are told they need.

It is easy to get carried away with appliances. The small ones make good gifts and come into the house spontaneously for the most part. Human inventiveness has produced something electrical for every purpose, from cooking a hot dog to shining a shoe or shuffling a deck of cards. Additional television sets easily accumulate as a new appliance is brought in and the old one relegated to a bedroom. And up goes the cost. It costs money to operate a small appliance and even more for the larger ones.

I once had an iron, but with today's fabrics I no longer need it and have given it away. I have an electric kettle and a toaster, both left over from life in the city; I keep them for use when the kitchen stove is out preparatory to cleaning. I also have an electrical hot plate, which we use for processing vegetables for freezing on a summer day when a low fire in the cookstove is welcome.

Among the larger appliances, a freezer, clothes washer, vacuum cleaner, and electric blanket are essential. I used to think that a dishwasher was also essential, but having recently worn mine out, I do not intend to replace it. My family is small and I find I don't mind the old-fashioned dishpans that sit in my sink.

In a country home, the vacuum cleaner occupies a rather special place because so much of the outside comes inside. I can almost tell the season of the year by noting what accumulates on the kitchen floor. A brush-type broom will do the job, to be sure, but that means more dusting.

Some might suppose that an electric blanket is a luxury that might be dispensed with. True, maybe, but not when the temperature of one's bedroom is apt to get down to forty or fifty degrees. In winter we used to sleep on a feather bed with cotton flannel sheets, blankets, and a quilt on top of that. Also we would wear heavy night gear, including bed socks, and take along a couple of hot water bags. An electric blanket is much simpler.

When oil was cheap we did once consider having a furnace, but by that time we were accustomed to chunk stoves and it seemed easier to continue to use them. Then the price of oil went up and we discovered how fortunate we were. We had also noted how our friends who had installed furnaces after the war have complained thereafter of cold floors. We don't have that problem, although I don't really know why. It is probably something to do with the circulation of hot air coming from a chunk stove in the room it heats.

I must confess here that we do have several electrical baseboard units, but none are set higher than sixty degrees. There are three in the twelve-foot bay window area off the kitchen and another three in the bedroom where they are the only heat. One in the bathroom is seldom used.

One reason we can dispense with a furnace is that we find we do not have to heat the entire house in winter. The master bedroom and bath are on the ground floor. Two bedrooms upstairs are not regularly used. There is a chunk stove in each but not the kind that can be set for the day and then forgotten about. Being on the north side of the house, the guest room is especially cold, and it is an intrepid guest who knowingly agrees to occupy it in the winter. We sometimes store squash and onions there in winter, and they have been known to freeze. The upstairs bathroom is insulated and has its own electrical heating unit, turned off when not in use. My study is also on that floor but has a fine south window and a chunk stove that I use only when I need to.

If the winter is a really bitter one, we close off the living room and occupy the kitchen and the bay for general family living. The television is in the bay, which pleases those who watch organized sports. The long plant table in the bay window almost takes us outside, and a desk and bookcase provide a mellow atmosphere. A cold winter day with a snowstorm blowing outside makes this bay a cozy refuge. If the teakettle is singing on the stove and the aroma of a pot of stew is wafting toward the bay, most of the human senses are engaged in a single pleasurable episode that warms the heart and kindles the appetite.

As for gasoline, the nation has learned how to save it and so have we. Farmers can buy their gasoline at a discount but we use too little to make buying in bulk useful. Lawnmowers and chain saws are not heavy feeders. Modern road vehicles are now more fuel-efficient than they used to be, and we do not use gas-guzzlers.

The final type of energy in this list of fuels is wood, and the link between this fuel energy and human energy is the chain saw. If a rural household is dependent on a wood economy, as it should be, then the chain saw is its foundation.

Before the chain saw became available on a commercial basis after World War II, the crosscut saw, the ax, the maul, the splitting ax, and a set of wedges were all part of the pack that went into the woods for the purpose of bringing back a supply of firewood. Also included was the cant hook with which to maneuver logs. Most of these are still needed, except for the crosscut saw which is now obsolete. And it is a bit too bad, too. Many times I have stood on one end of a crosscut saw, my husband on the other, and pulled rhythmically as sharp teeth cut through a log. It was slow work to be sure, but there was a certain satisfaction to it, for the whole body was engaged. The sound was a gentle swish instead of the deafening sound of an unmuffled motor—no wonder the modern sawyer in the forest wears earmuffs. There was no need to hurry. The pace was slow, humanly slow, for to hurry was to exhaust oneself. Nor was there any smell, as of exhaust fumes. The job today is faster than formerly, and much more efficient in terms of man-hours, but the pleasures are fewer.

The operation was symbolized for me one day as I watched an elderly neighbor walk up the road with an ax over his shoulder. He passed our cottage where another neighbor, our farm partner, was in residence. Our partner came of of the cottage just as the man with the ax was passing. They hailed each other. "Going to chop down some trees?" asked the man on the stoop. "Heh, heh," replied the man with the ax, "going to chop some down and going to chop some up. Heh, heh." The man with the ax never paused in his stride, which was long and steady. So was the chuckle.

The chain saw is not the whole of the matter, for the wood must still be split, hauled, piled, seasoned, stacked in the woodshed, and finally brought into the house to fill woodboxes and other receptacles, which, in the course of a cold winter, seem to have an insatiable appetite all their own. It is here that human energy comes into the picture.

Human energy depends not only on nutrition—which is something more than calories—but also on exercise. Getting in a supply of wood provides its own exercise, as do many other activities in the country, including gardening, haying, filling silos, cutting grass (especially with a scythe), pruning trees, and bringing in the harvest. This is something the city dweller may appreciate from an intellectual point of view but has little chance to experience. In the country surely the setting has something to do with the quality of results. I sometimes see joggers in a city or on a campus determinedly getting their exercise, pounding their feet on pavement or a roadway, and no wood to show for it.

There is something almost addictive about getting in a wood supply. Filling a woodshed is a little like building up an account at the bank. Both represent hard and, it is hoped, useful work, fine exercise, and good winter warmth. A friend of ours who now lives in a town, has permission to cut wood for his chunk stove on another friend's woodlot. He sets himself a certain time limit and upon reaching it he deliberately stops work. Just one more stick, one more tree, or one more branch to be cleaned up. No, no. He forces himself to stop, to bring an end to the matter, to leave the rest for another day.

Working in the wood stimulates not only the body, but also the mind, the imagination, the perception of small things around you. A squirrel runs up the trunk of a tree; a porcupine eats the tender bark at the base of a sapling (in my husband's view, no worse crime). A deer may come to investigate, for deer are as curious as heifers and seem to know when there is no gun around. The sound of a saw seems to arouse this instinct. One notices how the trees are growing in response to good forest management, the cutting out of weed trees. One also notices how brooks and swamps appear in the spring and dry up, for the most part, in August. Then there are the many varieties of ferns and the places they grow: a mass of maidenhair here and Christmas fern there. Many varieties of wildflowers come up in the spring: carpets of spring beauties, dogtooth violets, the more shy hepaticas, the first to appear hiding under beds of last year's leaves. Jackin-the-pulpits and Solomon's seal. And carpets of violets: lavender, purple, yellow, and white.

At the suggestion of a painter friend, we have followed a policy in our woods of allowing certain ancient dead trees to remain as a kind of contrast to the main aspect of the forest. A big old dead maple with chopped-off arms, victims of age and the wind and rain, tells stories that can be interpreted with just a little imagination. We once had two enormous elms in the midst of our forest. They were giant guardsmen, and we left them in all their splendor, even when in due course they died of Dutch elm disease. Finally in a raging windstorm they came crashing down, no doubt shaking the forest floor as they acknowledged defeat. Elm wood is of little value as fuel unless it is thoroughly seasoned and gives little heat even then. So we left these old friends where they lay and each year have watched them return a little more into the soil, with ferns and moss growing onto them and finally, over them.

The best woods for burning, because they give the most heat, are the hardwoods. Hickory and oak are at the top of the list, but hickory does not grow around here and oak is scarce. We do have rock maple, yellow birch, beech, and ash. Soft maple is not much good, nor is white birch except for its pretty looks in a fireplace. Softwoods are good only for kindling.

Perhaps this is the place to explain how to make a fire in a chunk stove. In his long poem, "Snowbound," John Greenleaf Whittier says that to make a fire, in his case in a fireplace, one starts with a log against the back wall. In front of that one places kindling, and two more logs crossed. One log is hard to kindle, two logs are better, but for some reason three are best. A physicist probably knows the reason for this; I know only that it works fine.

The same formula applies in a chunk stove. In the

more usual type of chunk stove, a back log is laid along the back wall under the stovepipe. In front of that plenty of crumpled newspaper is placed. The first section of the Sunday *New York Times* does fine and, in a sense, helps to defray the high cost of that edition of the paper. Kindling is added on top of the paper. Split, dry pine boards (refuse from a sawmill) are easy to acquire but must be split fine. On top of the kindling go two smaller logs, split if possible since these take hold of the fire easier than unsplit pieces. The draft of the stove must be clear of ashes behind it. This is done with a poker. After applying a lighted match, one waits until the kindling sparks and then adjusts the draft, closing it about half way as a rule. And there you have a fire.

It is always easier to make a fire on hot ashes than in a cold stove. However, ashes must be taken out when they accumulate to the point of blocking the draft. Hot ashes when moved create dust, cold ashes do not. Ashes may be spread on lawn or garden, where they are good fertilizer except for root crops. Since chunk stoves are used principally in winter, hot ashes can be spread on the snow without danger of starting an unwelcome fire.

To keep a chunk stove going for most of the night, I put in one or two heavy, unsplit logs before going to bed and close the draft—also the damper in the pipe, just above the stove. With the proper grates, this same night-time procedure works in the kitchen stove as well. By the proper grates I mean open ones through which ashes can easily fall. Some stoves have a plate with a row of small holes along one side. In this case ashes must be scraped through the holes each morning (this works best if the fire is out).

Heating with wood fires has yet another advantage, and that is in the quality of the ions produced. The ions from artificial heat, such as oil and electric, produce positive ions which react negatively on the human nervous system. One becomes nervous, jumpy, and uncomfortable. It has something to do with the inorganic nature of the fuel, and heating engineers are aware of it. Organic fuel such as wood, on the other hand, produces negative ions, creating a comfortable feeling, a feeling of relaxation that is immediately noticeable when one enters a room that is heated with wood. To walk into our kitchen from the cold outside is to experience this feeling of soothing warmth, on which those unaccustomed often remark.

A final advantage of wood fires is the ease of cooking on a wood-burning cookstove. I have used many gas and electric stoves and none compares, in ease of cooking, with a wood burner. The chief advantage is the lack of one-spot heat. Rather, it is a diffused heat, with the hottest spot over the firebox and decreasing heat as one moves away from it. There is little danger of burning unless one leaves a pot on the hot spot for too long. Once the cooking has been completed, the pot can be moved to a cooler area and left for as long as needed, overnight if you like. A teakettle is always hot, sometimes singing, and ready for that occasional cup of tea or coffee. Nothing needs close watching except the fire, and one soon learns not to neglect it. The oven is always hot, no preheating required. And while all this is going on, or not going on, the stove is quietly heating all of your household water. If, that is, you have what is called a water front in your firebox hitched to a hot water tank.

With these advantages of wood heat, there is no greater satisfaction than to spend a day in the woods, come home to a warm kitchen, take a shower, perhaps partake of one's favorite libation, and then sit down to a good dinner for which most of the food has been home-produced and all of it home-cooked, and to eat it in comfort and warmth. Such delights must be experienced to be fully appreciated. So many people have no idea that they even exist.

Yet another aspect of human energy is sleep. And what better way to prepare for it than to be physically relaxed after a day of work in the woods, garden, or fields, or even the study. Physically tired, emotionally relaxed, and well-fed is the prescription for a good night's sleep. That old bogey having to do with long winter evenings is a myth. I have asked many friends around here if they have ever encountered a long winter evening, and none ever has. Especially in recent years when television fills all empty time, or anyhow occupies it.

Bed calls early in country life, and so does morning. What is so sweet as five o'clock in the morning on a spring day, with birds singing and a gentle breeze bringing the scent of the earth, of apple blossoms, and the firewood piled in the shed. Bed practically throws you out of it and into the adventures of the day.

Vermont is known for the longevity of its people. I once commented to a local doctor, a native of Korea, that I had recovered quickly from a broken leg because of the fine simple life we lead here. To that he replied, "That is why I am here." And a little while ago I discovered that although I have had diabetes for more than forty years, I have outlived my projected life span by a number of years. No surprise to me, because I feel not much older than I did twenty years ago. It must be that good simple life-style that comes naturally in a country setting.

13

Health

IT HAS BEEN SAID THAT IN VERMONT, IF YOU WANT TO START A cemetery, you have to shoot somebody. Out of curiosity, having noticed the large proportion of senior citizens around here, I started paying closer attention to the vital statistics for this area as printed in the local weekly newspaper. And sure enough, most people died in their seventies, eighties, or even nineties. When I first started reading them, the death columns were not very long, and if anybody died before the age of seventy it was unusual. Such deaths were most often from acute illness or accident. These days longevity is no longer so common because more short-lived people are coming in from the outside, and in addition the so-called benefits (stresses) of civilization are now as popular here as elsewhere.

I once took a horse to a neighbor's country blacksmith shop to have a shoe reset. Lew, the smith, and I fell to discussing the death of a mutual friend, the man who owned the local hardware store. "Too young," said Lew. I agreed. "But the thing that gits me," said Lew, "is that it's peckin' pretty close to me." Lew was seventy-two and had celebrated his fiftieth wedding anniversary the previous year. "And old enough to sign my own weddin' license, too," he commented with some pride. Lew had also survived cancer of the jaw and his face was askew. But his wit was sharper than ever. "They tried to git me, but they couldn't," he had said when he came home from the hospital.

I didn't realize until quite a bit later that longevity and good health are a sewn-in part of a country life-style. Now I understand that they are a combination of many factors, all of which interrelate here in the country. These include diet, environment, and hard work. One grows one's own fresh or freshly preserved food. One's animals have been cleanly fed and one's vegetables have had no commercial fertilizer. In other parts of the country it is also possible to produce one's own grain. With all this fresh food, diet is a matter of tradition and choice. It used to be that most farm meals in Vermont consisted of meat and potatoes, partly because keeping a garden took a good deal of time and partly because many disdained vegetables as "rabbit food." But I know one farm woman who grew and canned seventy quarts of peas in one season, and another who picked and canned eighteen pints of wild strawberries in a single June. Even farm families know more about diet these days, and habits have changed.

Vitamins are also a matter of choice. Some do and some don't. For the most part vitamins are not needed, but sometimes they are, especially for the elderly and for those who are ill. Much information is available on the subject— I don't intend to discuss it here! Then there is the factor of exercise, achieved in the production of one's own food and firewood, to say nothing of much walking in the course of the daily round from house to barn to fields and forest. A neighbor of ours used to take a long walk at the end of every afternoon, up into high pastures. She was not out for fun but to bring in the cows to be milked. They did not seem to have the instincts of some cows I have known, which brought them to the pasture gate at milking time.

Rather, one had to search for them and drive them, with the aid of a dog, to their routine destination.

Also, there lacks the stress that results from driving in traffic, being subject to much noise and polluted air, and wasting time in long lines, all of which are common factors in urban or suburban life. And finally at the end of the day, there is quiet, comfortable sleep, after going to bed as early as you like, and inevitably and joyously waking up with the sun—often enough to the sound of birds rather than the sound of the garbage truck.

A final part of the overall pattern of health in the country is reduction of those insidious sorts of stress that one barely notices, but which pile up all the same. A back road does not have what one can call traffic. The school bus and an occasional car or truck are about it. Even on the blacktop into town traffic is local and minimal. Parking in a town our size is no problem. Noise there is pretty much limited to the sound of the train going through our valley on its way to Montreal, a sound so nostalgic for some of us as to be a delight. Local merchants are all friends and to shop in their stores is a friendly, welcoming occasion. Nor are the local supermarkets all that crowded. Waiting in a doctor's or dentist's office is more pleasant than otherwise, because the people there are folks whom you have known for some time and you spend a pleasant interlude comparing news and exchanging gossip. Gossip has a malicious connotation, but I have never heard that kind in our area. Generally the gossip to which I refer is a matter of concern for someone, or pleasure at their good fortune. It is catching up on who is doing what and how the kids are getting along in school.

Such stress as is encountered in the country has its own therapy. Working in the garden, for example, is an excellent way to get rid of your frustrations and irritations.

Complications in the household can be profitably worked off by spreading mulch around the tomatoes or by weeding the carrots. Here you can forget about problems in the family, and by the time you get back to them they have assumed their proper, minimal proportions. I know a woman whose husband was not as sharp as she, and when she was irritated by his sometimes slow response, her favorite therapy was to go out to her rose garden and spend the afternoon caring for her plants. It worked every time.

And gardening provides one of the best kinds of exercise, too, because you are on your knees, or sitting on the ground and stretching forward and to the sides, or standing with hoe or pitchfork to spread mulch, or bending over, "rumping it," as an elderly friend used to call it. You may not think of the exercise part of the occupation, so intent are you on the more interesting aspects of gardening, but it is there all the same and, if you are a good cook, doing wonders for that little tendency to gain weight.

Much heavier exercise is found working in the woods: felling trees, working them up, loading them in a rig of some kind, hauling them to the shed, splitting and piling them, and eventually bringing them into the house. Loading and then unloading a haywagon used to be a strenuous form of exercise during the summer, and handling bales of hay can be hard work. Increasingly, however, there is specialized and very expensive machinery to accomplish these tasks. The same is true for the harvesting of corn or hay silage, but unless the subsistence farmer is helping a neighbor on a commercial farm such tasks do not often come his or her way.

Those who have never tried it can scarcely realize the delights of a day of work at one's own pace, chores among friendly animals, a good dinner, a final inspection of the

116

garden, and then to bed for a long night of relaxed sleep, in a state of deep quiet.

There are, of course, hazards to be found in rural life. One of the main threats to the health of a country person is the possibility of accident. People coming from the city or the suburbs are especially vulnerable because often they do not anticipate the possibility of what could go wrong with the new kinds of tools they may be using for the first time. Some tools may be lethal to the unwary, especially the tractor and the chain saw.

While a tractor is a versatile piece of machinery that does not keep eating its head off while standing in a stall, it still must be approached cautiously. For a swashbuckler on a tractor with an inadequate sense of balance, driving on the side of a hill is quite apt to cause some problems. Some tractors turn over more easily than one might suppose and the consequence is a long stay—under the sod, in the hospital, or, at best, in the house. Even experienced farmers can misjudge a slope. What a tractor consumes in the fuel, plus its maintenance, plus its original cost, should lead the subsistence farmer to take a hard look at the financial outlay before deciding to buy. To resist the persuasions of the salespeople will be hard, but go slow anyhow. If you do buy a tractor, read the instructions and take it easy at first.

A neighbor of ours had spent most of his life farming but had never got the hang of driving a loaded haywagon on the side of a hill. For one thing, he was just plain stubborn and refused to let that hill get the better of him. So every few years he turned his haywagon over on its side, the downhill side, much to the confusion of his horses and at the cost of much hard swearing on his own part. (They sometimes call that "hard labor plus much calling on the Lord.")

Some people have a sense of balance and some don't.

Piling wood in your shed calls for the exercise of this instinct. A stack of wood may go up quite nicely for a while, only to tumble for no apparent reason. Take a good look at it, try to get the feel.

For its part, a chain saw must also be used with knowledge and caution. It is a dangerous weapon. If the chain hits a knot in a log, or a nail or a tap in an old maple, the blade will jump or buck, causing a nasty wound. Marshall's boots show some unpleasant scars, and I have been glad his toes were steel-protected. Sometimes the chain will break and wrap itself around a portion of the unwary person. Therefore, chains must be carefully and regularly inspected. In all of these circumstances the first rule is observation and the second is caution. If you are not sure, ask someone who is.

Then there are bulls. Now that artificial insemination is common, the herd sire is no longer much of a menace, but in times past this animal presnted quite a challenge. My elderly blacksmith friend who was also a farmer once told me of leading his bull to water in a yard across the road from his barn. While the bull was drinking, Lew incautiously turned his back to speak with a neighbor over the fence. Next thing he knew he had been hoisted by the bull's head over the fence and found himself sitting in the middle of the road. Lew and the neighbor managed to drive the excited animal back into the barn. The next day he hitched a bull staff to the ring in the bull's nose and led him out to water. Halfway there the bull put his head down, "drilled a furrow down the middle of the road with a horn, tore the ring out of his nose, and took off," Lew reported. Again he was driven back to the barn where he then stayed for the rest of his useful life. But his water came by the bucket. Finally one day Lew, with rifle in hand, climbed up to a high beam in his barn. Then his neighbor opened the door to the bull stall, and with much pleasure

Lew put a bullet between the bull's horns. That skull stayed in the neighborhood for many years and may still be around if one were to look for it.

Horses also can cause injury if you are not accustomed to their ways. They have a nasty habit, for example, of striking out with a forefoot when you happen to be incautiously standing in front of them. Always stand to the side. A blow from a front hoof can be harder than a blow from the rear, as I have reason to know by experience. And beware of being hit on the backside by a tough old ram.

Also in the matter of accidents, those caused by the automobile are always with us, wherever we live. But there are fewer cars in the country, which helps a little. In the country, furthermore, accidents more often result from bad roads, ice, slipping into a ditch, than from encountering another car. Speed is less of a factor, especially during hunting season when many drivers are alert for the sight of a buck and drive with that in mind. Another factor is that back roads are not conducive to speed anyhow, although as these roads are gradually improved, speeds do increase. (We would almost rather have bad roads.)

Accidents in the woods, such as heart attacks, falls, and accidental shootings pick up quite a bit during hunting season. In our part of the country, regular legal deer season is sometimes supplemented by a so-called antlerless season, when the taking of does and even fawns by bow and arrow is permitted. No side arms permitted. These arrows are highly dangerous, however. The tips are some two or three inches long, made of sharp raw steel. Once during doe season I was sitting in a doctor's waiting room along with four or five other patients. We all knew each other and were happily catching up on the news. I was by a window and saw a red Jeep pull up to the curb. A rather large young man dressed in camouflage—the standard costume for the bow-and-arrow hunter—got out and came into the doctor's office. In the waiting room he had a whispered consultation with the receptionist, who went into the doctor. She returned and told the young man to bring his friend in. He went out and returned with his pal, also in full camouflage but leaning over and obviously in some pain. The nurse showed them into the consulting room and came out giggling. It seems, she said, that when he was getting over a fence he stuck himself in the buttocks with his own arrow. We all had a good laugh at the expense of this greenhorn. I still can't figure out how he could have done such a thing, for it must have taken some ingenuity. The town grapevine had spread the tale before nightfall.

Illnesses occur in the country as well as elsewhere, of course, but there seem to be fewer here than in the city. Or used to be, at any rate, before the influx of people seeking refuge among our green hills, although I suspect the same conditions prevail in other country areas. With increasing population, the rate of illnesses seems also to have increased, although not so much as might be expected statistically.

The means of coping with illness have also greatly increased. Where once a few small regional hospitals sufficed, now there are two large university teaching hospitals within driving distance, plus one medical center with first-rate facilites. One way or another these hospitals and the smaller ones have affiliated to form a network of services. The smaller hospitals are by far the nicest, for one knows many of the staff and patients.

I sometimes wonder if all the new medical technology being developed by hospitals isn't a question of installing the equipment and then looking for enough patients on whom to use it in order to pay for it.

In our town there is also a group of medical associates with their own out-patient facilities, if this is enough, and ready access to hospitals if it is not. In addition we have an ambulance service, local rescue squads, at least two home nursing services, and numerous hospice arrangements. County facilities are available for the mentally ill, plus a state hospital for this purpose when all else fails.

There are a number of nursing homes in the area, plus a home helping service whereby people aid the elderly and the handicapped in their household chores, and keep an eye on their health as well. Thus many of the elderly and infirm are able to live at home, even alone if necessary, for much of the time instead of going to a nursing home.

As I already mentioned, in a small community such as ours there is a remarkably efficient and speedy grapevine, and everyone knows the best ways to tap into it. Thus no one in trouble such as illness is without help when it is needed. And even when it isn't. We all know each other in a small community, doctors and patients included. There is a story told, which I confirmed, that on one occasion a local doctor was called to the home of a farmer who was ill. The farmer was so sick that the doctor proposed to take him to the hospital at once. But the farmer refused, saying that his cows had not been milked and he would have to do that first. The doctor went to the barn forthwith and milked the cows himself, alerted a neighbor, and then took the stubborn farmer to the hospital. In cases such as this the neighbors gather round and do the necessary for as long as need be. The man's cows were in good hands.

If proof of the pudding is needed that one's overall health is better in the country than in the city, I can cite our own case. My husband, for example, is now a vigorous eighty-one. He does not do quite the heavy physical work as formerly but his mind is sharper than ever. In his field, which is political science, he is virtually dean and elder statesman. He does his barn chores, taking care of the chickens and pigs, works in the garden, and now that I am blind does all the household errands. Since he has cataracts he drives a Jeep instead of a car, for it provides better visibility, and he is able to get to town in all kinds of weather and over all kinds of roads.

As for me, I learned a few years ago that I have outlived my life expectancy as a juvenile-onset diabetic. Outlived it by quite a few years, in fact, but I was so surprised by the news that I forgot to ask by how many years. At seventy-six I doubt it matters much, except as a matter of curiosity. I did not lose my sight until age sixty-eight, after a lifetime of very good vision, extensively used. So I have no complaints. What lies ahead offers a number of interesting and, to me, rewarding challenges.

I have a feeling that like happiness, health is a by-product of what one does and how one lives.

14

Community

ONE OF THE MOST SATISFYING ASPECTS OF LIVING YOUR OWN life in the country is getting to know the local community and taking an active part in its affairs. In the city this opportunity is either lacking or ignored. Seldom does one meet one's neighbors or even know the names of those living in the same apartment building. Community groups do exist in the city, especially groups associated with the churches or private clubs. But in my opinion the quality of these is a far cry from the quality of groups in a semirural environment. In the suburbs the situation is a little better, but there the women are chiefly involved, because most of the men live there only on a part-time basis.

By contrast, a country community is made up of full-time residents with varied occupations and interests, all of whom depend to some degree on their fellow citizens. People come to know each other, in person or by name or reputation. A network of interrelationships unites the community around particular issues, interests, activities, concerns, crises, and occupations.

In these congeries of circumstances, the two words that best describe the characteristics that prevail are caring and privacy. Everyone knows the other fellow's business, and often more than that. But no one intrudes on his fellows, for privacy is respected. After so many years in this community, I know a gread deal about a great many people, often at second hand—which means that people talk about each other. Yet I have never heard really malicious gossip from anyone.

Perhaps the most satisfying thing about being part of a local community is the sense of belonging one gains from it. Unobtrusively it surrounds you, and when you need it, as you will, it is there with strength and support. Sometimes one needs only the feeling of support, and it is there. For example, several years ago when my sight began to fail and of course everyone in town knew it, I felt sympathy and concern on every hand. And when finally I became blind, I felt the sense of caring whenever I appeared on the main street or in the shops. People went out of their way to help and to convey their sympathy by a hand on my arm, an extra special handshake, a cheery question.

I too have found myself a part of that type support for someone in trouble. A woman I did not know very well but who belonged to a group of which I was a member, lost her husband. A month or two later I ran across her in a store in a neighboring town. I spoke her name and put a hand on her arm. She looked around, put her arms around me and without a word, we embraced. Then she went back to her conversation with the clerk behind the counter and I waited my turn. On another occasion, Marshall and I were guests at a Christmas party at the home of a friend. A guest's father, of whom we were very fond, had recently died, and I had written the daughter a note of heartfelt sympathy. When a number of us at the party gathered around a piano to sing carols, she was there. She saw me and came over, put her head on my shoulder for a moment, and then resumed singing. We were not close friends, but there was a common bond that we both understood.

As a final illustration, there was an older woman in town whom everyone respected and loved. She had a friend whom all expected her to marry, but she didn't. He became terminally ill and died, but because she was a very private person who did not speak much of herself, no one spoke to her openly about this tragedy in her life. But one could feel the whole town thinking of her, surrounding her with sympathy and concern. And I am sure she felt it, too.

Concrete evidence of mutual caring occurs when a family home is burned, as happens now and then. It used to be that someone would volunteer to act as recipient of food, clothing, and furnishings for the family in trouble. But now that system has been reinforced by an organization called Neighbors Helping Neighbors. A store of food and clothing is kept at one of the churches to be used for these families and also for people who are down and out for reasons other than fire. On at least one occasion this organization rebuilt a house for a family, with donated help and materials.

When a family's barn burns, the time-honored procedure is for a neighbor to carry a "paper" around the neighborhood among the family's friends and the suppliers of building materials. One signs on to contribute building materials, a sum of money, or a pledge to work.

Not long ago a very old and dilapidated tenement building burned. It had housed twelve more or less poverty-stricken families including a good many children. It was nearly midnight in the midst of a cold winter, with snow on the ground, and some of the children were shoved outdoors to escape the flames, with no shoes on, standing panic-stricken in the snow. But as soon as the alarm sounded, the town mobilized. The wretched old building burned to the ground, but within two hours shelter among the townspeople had been found for everyone.

By the following day, clothing began to come in to the local community center, a former church building serving a compatible purpose. Clothing came from towns as far as forty miles away in such abundance that much of it was eventually passed along to other centers for the relief of the needy. On an informal basis, men and women showed up at the community center to sort clothing and to give help to those who needed it. Within two days the job was done.

Some people who take refuge in the country seek just that: refuge. Exhausted by the stresses of city life, they try to find a home as remote from the city and even from the local towns as possible. Some place on a hill, in a clearing in the woods, with symbolic protections and barriers between them and civilization. People who have lived in the comfortable but arid circumstances of bedroom towns seek privacy in the country, even isolation, no matter how impractical that may turn out to be. The farther away from other people the better. They don't realize that in a rural setting, people depend on one another and get satisfaction out of offering and receiving help, without any sense of obligation. That is how it is, and to ignore it is to lose something that is good and real and necessary.

It is all right, even desirable, to live in a remote area so long as one establishes ties with the community, for in this way the advantages of country living are multiplied. It is also desirable under certain circumstances to buy a place in a small town or village, especially if one is getting on in years. For one thing, one does not need a car, because everything is within walking distance—and there comes a time when to drive a car is not convenient. Also one is closer to other people when help is needed, and closer to church, to group meetings, and to stores. And closer, too, to friends who drive cars and who think of you when they are going to a more remote shopping center or going on an errand in some other town. A retired school teacher, widowed, now spends the summer and fall in her own home in our town. She has been retired for many years, but each Halloween she welcomes more than a hundred young people at her door and distributes treats. She knows them all by name, though for the most part they are now the children of former pupils. If anything happened to her, the whole town would know it and help as much as needed.

There is nothing wrong with abstaining from community life, or withdrawing from it for a period of time. The English philosopher-historian Arnold Toynbee once said that withdrawal is to be encouraged if the urge is there, that an active person may seek a period of withdrawal from his usual concerns in order to renew himself. This period of withdrawal may last for a short while or for several years. During this time the person will continue to work but in a different occupation than before. His or her work during this time will be productive. However, if the person then returns to his or her former occupation, he or she will be even more productive than in the past. Withdrawal and return are the means of enhancing creativity for the individual. It is a little like the French proverb "reculer pour mieux sauter," meaning to retreat in order to jump the better.

In a country setting, to make withdrawal a permanent state would be a mistake, because involvement in the community is a creative thing in itself. So much can be given with so little effort, and it will be noticed. Even more, so much is received by the individual in terms of human relations, perspectives, insights, and fellow feeling.

There are many ways to become active in the community. Years ago we learned that in our town of some fifteen hundred inhabitants, of whom nine hundred lived in the village, there were sixty different organizations. And in a neighboring town of little more than two thousand inhabitants, the number of organizations was ninety. The groups range from the formal such as the women's club and Rotary, to the informal, almost ad hoc groups set up for a particular purpose and quietly disbanded when interest flags.

The easiest way to become involved in the community is to join one of these groups. Easiest of all is to join or attend a church. Almost all churches have groups for women, sometimes for men, and usually for young people as well. From such affiliations, the members branch out to other groups, crisscrossing, interchanging, and increasing their alliances until the whole town seems like a web of fanning out, crossing lines. Each group is different but all groups draw from the same reservoir.

It is usual practice for a newcomer in our town to try out the various churches, of which we have four. The differences between denominations seem slight, except for the Catholic church. If one is a Catholic one joins that church, but among the non-Catholics it is a matter of choice, not a permanent one. Moreover, our town is known as an ecumenical town because the four churches join in many activities.

It was noted, for example, that when each church held its own annual fair to meet its annual budget, none of the churches made very much. A woman we knew used to make an apron to her own specifications, take it to the Methodist fair, and buy it back. Then she would take the same apron to the Episcopalian fair, then to the United Church fair, and finally to the Catholic fair. By that time she had contributed to each group and wound up with an apron she liked.

Then someone came up with the idea of combining all of the fairs into one. Adequate space was found in a former church that is now a community center. So we formed an organization, assigned responsibilities for the various tables and collections, created a method of accounts, had a lot of fun working together, and made four or five times as much money for each church than we had in the past. The Four Church Fair has become well-known for its sale items, including antiques, which we haul out of our attics. A real bonanza occurs when someone dies during the year and we get an accumulation from perhaps several lifetimes.

In a small, indigenous town are all manner of people and occupations. There is even a kind of social rank depending on age of the family, private wealth, and the like, but none of it makes any difference in social acceptability, something that flatlanders do not always understand. They sometimes assume that their own values are superior—or that they themselves are superior. The local people are quick to recognize this. If the "superior" persons are incapable of looking after their own interests, then a local person feels free to take advantage of them.

We avoided this trap when my husband set out one day to spread manure. He loaded and off-loaded twelve truckloads single-handedly. This became known, and the next year he was asked to represent the town in the state legislature. The local farmers supported him on the strength of his manure-spreading prowess.

People of all ranks mingle equally, belong to the same groups, and are respected for what they can do. No one tries very hard to step up to a higher rank, because all have equal dignity and receive equal respect. All work, and all work is honorable.

There are the lodges and their ladies' auxiliaries. There are organizations for professional groups such as school teachers and, in conjunction with adjoining towns, there are organizations for lawyers, health care professionals, ministers, parents, young marrieds (in our town called the Hoppin' Housewives), and the like. There are also local chapters of larger organizations such as the Freemasons and other lodges, Alcoholics Anonymous, and the American Association of University Women. There are groups such as Senior Citizens, DAR, quilt makers, actors and singers, musicians, scouts, and librarians. There are groups for outdoor activities such as horseback riding, snowmobiling, bicycling, hiking, and even exploring former back roads (that are now little more than trails). For the latter a Jeep is necessary, and if the Jeep has a winch, so much the better. These former roads are known as "thrown up," meaning that they are no longer maintained. The description is often accurate.

Almost any group with a common interest can organize on an informal basis and continue as long as the interest lasts. The membership in these groups is composed of many people from other groups. Some people may belong to one or two groups, others to half a dozen or more. The source is the population of the town plus that of neighboring towns. By belonging to several groups one may meet the same people over and over again. Close relationships develop on the basis of these shared interests.

Other groups having to do with local government are in a different classification, although they still draw from the same source. In much of New England, in part of New York State, and occasionally elsewhere, the primary source of local government is the town meeting. It is the only example of true direct democracy left in the United States, and we honor it as such. Once a year, regularly, and more often if necessary, the people of a town gather to do the town's business or to authorize it. All citizens of the town may attend, and all names on the grand list may vote. The annual town report has been distributed; this includes a statement of the year's activities, the budgets for both the past year and the coming year, and the agenda for the present meeting. The officers, including those whose terms are expiring, are also noted in the report. If the incumbents cannot be persuaded to continue in office, new officers will have to be elected. In some cases, this is not so easy a job. . . . Issues such as local policy, purchases of new equipment, and how to manage the water system or the sewage system are up for discussion.

Town meetings may be held during the day or at night and continue until the agenda is completed. In our town the meetings are held in the morning and break for lunch (which is put on in the school cafeteria by a local group for a benefit). Then back to the meeting. The regular town meeting is followed by a meeting of the local school district—an important event because most of the town's taxes go for schools.

Any citizen may run for any school or town office and, if he or she is willing to serve and has the qualifications needed, can usually be elected, unless for some reason he or she has incurred the wrath of voters who resent his or her actions in this matter or that. If a citizen fails to show up and speak his or her mind, then he or she must take the consequences.

Town officers serving without pay include three to five selectmen, one of whom is elected chief. They may have a town manager, a trained professional who is paid a salary and serves at the selectmen's pleasure. The town clerk is a vital officer, whose responsibilities include keeping records and selling licenses (hunting, fishing, dog, and the like). There is also a collector of taxes and a town agent, usually a lawyer.

Then comes a series of officers such as pound keeper, tree warden, fence viewer, cemetery commissioner, and so on. Listers, really assessors, hold an important job. So does the road commissioner. One can blame a lot of things on these officers.

In addition, there are a number of separate organizations also having to do with government: planning boards, tax grievance commissions, zoning commissions, school boards, and library boards. It is sometimes hard to persuade busy citizens to take the time to serve on these boards, but those who do are rewarded with interesting work and the gratitude, often unexpressed but nevertheless understood, of their fellow citizens.

With so much going on it is often hard to find a free day or evening to set up a new activity in order to raise money for a particular purpose—a food sale, a rummage sale, a supper, or a bazaar for a given cause.

Today there is a growing interest in volunteer work and the opportunities are constantly increasing. Hospitals are always in need of such assistance. In addition there are senior citizens, day-care programs, schools needing teachers' aides, blood drawing clinics, libraries, and the church programs. Indeed, almost any interest of the average citizen and his or her newcomer friends can be put to work for the good of many and the sure satisfaction of those who contribute.

In this network of community groups the question of recreation is at least partially solved. Many groups have recreation as an objective, such as bowling, tennis, or snowmobiling. Add to these the sports programs of the local high school, which are of interest all year but seem to reach a high point in winter when basketball is the subject of almost impassioned interest. Add to these a concert, a minstrel show, a barbecue roasting of a full-size steer, and in our case, a takeoff on the *Hee Haw* television show, which each year raises a good-size sum for a benefit and provides the pleasure of roasting some of the town's better-known citizens as well.

Then there are pet shows, hobby shows, craft shows, flower shows, and more. The variety seems endless and is always interesting.

A fine example of how the members of a community can join together for a given purpose took place in our town when a piece of land, formerly part of the town common, became available. There had been a school on it for seventy years. Then the school was damaged by fire, a new school was built elsewhere, and the question became: What is to be done with the remains? The matter was complicated by the loss of an old deed, mislaid by the school board and never registered in the town clerk's office. So presumably the land remained in the former ownership, a church across the street.

Should this land be occupied by a professional building, or by a builder of organs (one such would like to acquire it), a supermarket, a community center, or a parking lot? Or should the common be restored? The church held some leverage and exercised it. The lot was in a residential part of town, so the commercial plans were criticized. Eventually most of the town took an interest in the matter. The consensus favored restoration of the common; plans were drawn at cost by an outside consulting firm, to include a sunken garden within the foundations of the old school. Costs were determined, and the whole plan was minutely discussed at a well-attended special town meeting, and unanimously approved. Donations came in, a bequest was received, and much of the work was contributed or done at cost. Today it is a lovely site maintained by the women's clubs, the Boy Scouts, the Rotary, and the town. Occasional beer cans are quickly scooped up and disposed of by vigilant citizens. The common is the backdrop for weddings, fairs, and concerts; a fine addiiton to the town; and a source of satisfaction for all who helped to make it come about.

With all of the close relationships in the community, there is also abiding respect for the privacy of the individual. This is at least as rewarding as the close relationship encountered in common efforts. People need privacy for themselves and respect it in others. Privacy is never total, of course. After more than forty years here we have many friends of long standing. We have been in each other's homes; it is common to stop in for a cup of coffee or to exchange information or to collect for a cause. Relationships can be strengthened this way, but that is not the purpose of the visit. It just happens and both parties are the richer for it. Formal calling is at a minimum; I have never been to a formal ladies' luncheon around here, and only a few times to an informal dinner or cocktail party in a private home. Nor have we had many of our own. Larger parties take place now and then, planned around Christmas, a birthday, an anniversary. There are also neighborhood parties with as many as forty or fifty participants. Each guest brings a contribution to the dinner and the bar. All kinds of things get discussed, a small ball game may get underway. Nothing is organized except the food of which there is always a surplus by some of the best cooks in the county. Such parties are a spontaneous rather than formal affair, but they may happen each year at about the same time, depending on how well the haymaking is going or the corn for the silo is maturing.

How does culture come into this system? By many means, increasingly available. Every small town has its library, for instance, hooked into the state system and its exchanges. Local concerts and state symphonies are regular. Some movie houses are still around, though not many of them show the better films. Public broadcasting stations on radio and television are increasingly plentiful, with an abundance of music, news, forums, and discussions from all parts of the country on a variety of subjects. Newspapers and periodicals on every conceivable subject are as common in the country as in the city. Colleges and universities are never very far away even in the more remote areas of the land. Their libraries, courses, and cultural offerings are available to the Vermont public. The state university and college system offers a multitude of courses in small towns, not only for the convenience of local teachers, who must continually upgrade their own education, but also for Vermont residents who need to complete degree work or who would initiate it. Programs are offered by the state that make possible the attainment of a high school diploma. The winter adult educational program even includes fun courses ranging from rug hooking to aerobic dancing and carpentry to Chinese cooking, which proliferate like spring flowers and are just as welcome through the long, cold season. Local concerts and plays are often very good and are always fun to work with. Lectures arranged by Rotary or the local historical society are also interesting. And failing all else, especially on a blustery winter evening with the snow falling and the wind rising, we come again to books. Or television, if that is your thing—and even that may include programs coming under the heading of culture.

A favorite summer activity is to attend a flower show or an exhibition by local artists. There is always a lot of interest here. Perhaps you didn't know your neighbor was a quiet worker in a studio. Pottery is another occupation that combines well with a flower show.

Many small towns have a museum sponsored and maintained by the local historical society. It is fun to set up a museum, to arrange lectures and exhibits, and to attend museum functions with your friends, especially if one of the exhibits contains a piece you have contributed. Some people maintain their own private museums, as in one case I know of where an interest in semiprecious stones turned a small henhouse into a museum. It was situated in what had become a lavish garden, and the path leading to it was bordered with tuberous begonias, a lush plant of many opulent colors.

A final point is that if cultural opportunities in the country are less than in the city, you will find that when you get a chance to visit the city you will more fully appreciate the cultural opportunities you find there.

I have observed, and it is no doubt true in other places, that the town we live in is just the right size to constitute an active and involved community. Its population of just fifteen hundred makes it possible for most people to be identified by their neighbors. In larger towns, because of rifts and schisms, or this issue or that policy, there is a degree of backbiting and malicious gossip. Among the young, vandalism is not uncommon. Not so when people know each other better and the community is more fluid within itself. Antagonism occurs, to be sure, but it is confined to issues and not to people. The quickest way to lose one's influence is to attack a fellow citizen in public, as through a letter to the editor or a denunciation at a public meeting. But so long as conflicting views are centered on issues, people will listen and reach their own judgments without letting animosity get in the way.

I have also observed that in a small community values and mores are continued from one generation to the next through a common understanding that may be quite special to a given community. When we first came here there was an older generation who served as a guide for our behavior. We, who were younger then, looked up to the older people, either asking for their advice or following their example. As the town clerk remarked to us, "You aren't familiar with the local mores, but you know they're there, and you respect them." Now that generation has stepped out, and we find that we are the "wise old seniors." Thus is the continuity preserved; we count this one of the main advantages of life in a small community.

15

Outside Income

THERE REMAINS A FINAL QUESTION ABOUT A RURAL LIFE-STYLE. How do you pay for it?

Nothing in the preceding chapters implies that you can afford to live in the country simply by living there. Here, as in the city, there must be a ready supply of cash to pay for all the things we are told we must have and that by now we sincerely think we need. Subsistence farming has become an aspect of a rural life-style, but it is no longer an adequate basis for economic survival. Something more is usually needed, and there are more possibilities than one might suppose.

So what do you do for money?

It bears repeating that anyone considering commercial farming starting from scratch is crazy, because there is no way to succeed except under the most favorable conditions. These are increasingly rare in this part of the country, although less so in the great farming areas in the Middle West and West. Truck farming, on the other hand, in many parts of the country is a good source of income, especially if you like gardening. I know from experience that in some cases gardening can become much like an addiction. In this area it can also become quite profitable, especially as increasing numbers of people come here for the summer on a more or less regular basis. Such fugitives from the city often know little about gardening, care little for it, and in any case arrive too late to plant more than a few quick-growing vegetables like lettuce, radishes, and onion sets. In some parts of the country where the growing season is long, truck gardening can be really profitable. Here it is limited to about three months for ordinary purposes, which is about as long as the summer people last, too.

A good stand of raspberries or strawberries can be profitable on a pick-your-own basis. Other auxiliary products for those who like them are honey, maple syrup and sugar, plus apples, pears, and some varieties of plums. None of these, however, with the possible exception of apples, bring in enough profit for all of a family's needs.

So what does one do if the family coffers are not maintained by a steady flow of cash from investments or inheritance?

First, exercise your ingenuity. Look around and see what others are doing. Many young people with no prior training in any of the useful arts turn to carpentry as helpers to a master carpenter who knows the trade. But such a solution is not confined to the young. Men and women from different occupations may find that carpentry responds to a latent urge that can be developed to offer not only financial but also emotional rewards. There has been much building in recent years, plain and fancy: small structures, additions, restorations, and vacation homes.

Moreover, as one gains experience, carpentry can be combined with other home-building skills, such as masonry, plumbing, heating, electrical wiring, and even home decorating. Some of these skills can be learned on an apprenticeship basis, while others require some degree of formal training—not hard to come by. Such work can be done on a part-time, seasonal, or even permanent basis.

Men and women with some kind of previous professional training can often find financially useful positions in a rural community. Doctors, nurses, therapists, dentists, and other specialists in the health care field are in more or less constant demand resulting from turnover or expansion. It is often expensive to set up a practice in the medical field, especially in terms of equipment, but the increasing number of health centers and clinics help to solve this problem. A little ingenuity also helps, such as partnership arrangements and the like.

Lawyers are said to be becoming a surplus commodity throughout the nation, and this may be true for the more populated areas. In the country they are less numerous, although the rate is growing here, too, as young lawyers find enough work to keep them busy and provide them with a comfortable income and a more relaxed style of living. Our own area is becoming saturated with young lawyers, but for a special reason: Several years ago an independent law school was established in Vermont, and the school's graduates have a deep desire to stay here where life is less frantic than in the city. They are not without ambition, but it is on a manageable scale. Moreover, a legal training is the basis for many somewhat related occupations, such as politics, real estate, management, and insurance. Here, too, ingenuity will open new adventures in the art of making a living.

Then there is teaching, for which the demand is less than it used to be now that the baby boom generation is though college. Babies of the baby boom generation may soon change this situation. Although the monetary rewards of teaching are not great, teaching remains an attractive occupation, dealing as it does with the growing minds of young people. Combined with a rural life in a small community, teaching can become a life-style in its own right. In addition, there is a growing number of new specialties in this field that are proving attractive. There is special education, remedial reading, speech therapy, librarianship geared to the public schools, and counseling at a sophisticated level.

Another possibility is investment counseling and brokerage. One might not suppose that this type of occupation would have much potential in a small rural community. Some years ago I was told by a local broker that one would be surprised at how many well-stuffed socks were stashed away in Vermont's rural dwellings. By now these have come out of hiding, their contents invested and then managed by people who are knowledgeable and who offer professional assistance.

Banking also offers possibilities. So do retailing and the service trades. In these occupations, one typically starts as an assistant. Later it may be possible to start one's own business, except, of course, in banking. Even here, the path to the top for the determined individual may be a lot easier than in the city.

Real estate brokerage has been a lucrative business in many parts of the country. Despite serious setbacks resulting from recession, many such firms are small and can retrench along with decreased demand for quite a while before they must shut down. Mostly they endure the slumps for as long as they must and then revive as people continue to move to the country for at least part of the year. The element of ingenuity is especially needed here. Fortunately, in the country most people have command of many skills and can combine those skills in a number of interesting ways, so that when a primary occupation slows down, another can be brought up to supplement or even supplant it.

In the past, civil engineers have been in considerable demand as highways and especially the interstate system have become increasingly prominent. With the interstate system virtually completed, there continues a demand for maintenance of highways and bridges.

Rural areas in some parts of the country have encouraged light industries by granting concessions in the form of tax incentives and other services. Such industries include plastics, containers, building supplies, feeds and grains, small tools, and light garment manufacture. Many employ part-time workers, and housewives are quick to take advantage of this possibility. Thus they get away from housework for a while and bring in extra cash. A husband can't object to the one without objecting to the other as well, and this is hard to do.

If outside work is sought, much depends not only on ingenuity and imagination, but also on an appreciation of what is needed. What does the community lack that you can supply? Or, what need exists in the outside world that can be supplied from a rural residence? A man who was born in our town, fought in World War II, and returned here to make it his home again recognized a need—worldwide, as it turned out—that he could supply from here. He set up a brokerage in electrical wiring and cable. Most of the work was done by phone, which meant copious record keeping. Starting in a small suite of three or four rooms in a building on Main Street, he quickly occupied the whole building and then added a second building and warehouse for some of the wire that came through his brokerage. His telephone connections now reach into many parts of the world. The cables he deals in reach their destinations directly, from Brazil to Turkey, from Germany to Mexico, from Japan to India. Computers have now joined the telephone as a major part of the equipment he uses. All of his employees are local people, and he also makes room for people who need a job following hospitalization or some other disaster that has caused them to lose their original jobs. No one is surplus in his business and no one is useless. His enterprise from the start has been a success by any standard.

Other occupations that may be developed in the

country, either full or part time, are secretarial, custodial, security, household help, care of the elderly, horticulture, farm labor, preaching, custom trucking, working up lumber or firewood, forest management, custom tractor work, bulldozing, driving a school bus, blacksmithing, snowplowing, accounting, income tax preparation, teaching music and singing, electrical installation, electronic sales and maintenance, dog training, pottery, clerking, growing and selling herbs, making baked goods, dressmaking, machinist, house-sitting, babysitting, catering, and many more, as the opportunity is perceived.

In brief, find out what needs in the community are not met and try to meet them. The income from these sources, combined with reduced impulse spending, can produce a standard and the two add up to a balance at an optimum of living that's not high, but enough.

A significant difference between an urban life-style and a more simple rural culture seems to be that in the city one has a freewheeling attitude toward the spending of money. In the country, if one would save there is every opportunity to do so. This is partly because the opportunity to spend money is restricted, savings come easily, and the rewards thereof are tangible. An example is a young couple who were both born and raised in California but moved to Vermont in their early twenties. In California they seemed unable to save much money, although the incentive was there. In Vermont, where both were employed at lower salaries than formerly, they saved enough to make a down payment on a house in the first year. A modern, well-built house with a barn on ten acres, on the western slope of a friendly mountain, and on the outskirts of a small community. They were not quite sure how they managed to save that much money in one year, except that in the country they were less tempted to buy things they did not really need. Without being aware of it, they followed two rules that Vermonters observe: Do what you have to do, and make do with what you have.

Moreover, in some way that I have not figured out, there is a time factor here. Living in the country frees your time of many more or less compulsory but sterile activities inherent in an urban culture, and so you have more time to spend as you please. And some of that can be spent at a financial profit. In the city there is a great deal of moving about, driving two or three times a day when a single combined trip would do. Much standing and waiting, for a bus, in long lines, in finding parking space, and then walking to one's destination, getting to subways, and then getting out of them. Waiting your turn in a shop for attention, waiting for a waitress to serve you, and more. Because considerably less time is wasted in this manner if one lives in the country, it is like living a longer life in the course of a normal life span. This is partly because the quality of life in the country is better and more concentrated. Thus it seems as though one might live as much as twice as long in the country as in the city.

I can best explain this through my own experience, which after all is the one I know best: my husband, as I have already mentioned, is a professor of political science and also a writer on that subject. In college I majored in government and, by a kind of osmosis, can now claim to be a political scientist in my own right, although I lack a formal degree and have never taught. So he and I have compatible professional interests. By now Marshall has more than forty-five books to his name and I have been involved in all but a few as editor, rewriter, organizer, and on several of them, as coauthor. Marshall has also served as a federal official in labor, immigration, and shipping. He has been a consultant to many federal agencies, and almost as many large business corporations. He has served in a state legislature, the United Nations, and was the first

Moderator of the then newly combined Unitarian Universalist denomination.

Much of this has happened since we moved to the country, but the foundation was there much earlier. We had owned and intermittently used this place for seven years as an experiment in early retirement. For the next eight years we freelanced it, then Marshall accepted a fancy offer to return to full-time teaching. After five more years he retired again, at age fifty, and this time for good. Since then he has been busier than ever before with many more things than teaching.

We had supposed that there would be a period when we would be financially strapped, but this has not occurred. We have put four children through college and three of them through graduate school. In addition we have improved the place: we added-on to the house, built a separate study, maintained the cottage and barn, improved the pastures and meadows, built three drainage ditches in the meadows, planted more than two hundred thousand pines in what was once a scrub pasture, and improved the forest.

In addition we have done a great deal of traveling, which has been for professional assignments and not for sightseeing, although there has been much of this as a delightful by-product. There have been visiting professorships, usually for a semester at a time but once for a year in Japan. There was a United Nations assignment in Turkey for a year and a State Department mission in India for three months. There were two teaching jobs in Puerto Rico and one in England. Also, we spent nearly a year in England and on the island of Alderney to write a book. We have done well enough financially—at least to our own likes and standards. We do not buy fur coats or spend winter months in Florida, but we do have the luxury of staying home in a warm house, watching the changing seasons, eating our own food, and working our own home ground.

Marshall and I are now in our seventies, having arrived here almost without noticing what was happening to us in terms of age. I know for sure that it was only a year or so ago that suddenly I got a gut feeling that I am now elderly. I was surprised, like finding the first gray hair.

I now appreciate that after more than forty years in our own country home, with all the freedom of thought, motion, occupation, and travel it has afforded us, we have both lived several lifetimes. For each of us there was one lifetime spent in growing up, another spent in travel, a third as authors, and a fourth on our own home ground in the country. The last three have been lived concurrently, intermeshed, so to speak. But each one is a lifetime in itself and might have been lived separately. This probably could not have happened had we been born and bred in the city, educated there, worked there, and produced a family there.

At this point I feel as though we are standing on a promontory, surveying the past for the first time. Until now we have been occupied with the job at hand, seeing what needed to be done but not much aware of ourselves as individuals doing that job. It was on the job that counted, and for the most part the job has been worth the effort in terms of interest and adventure—meeting the job head-on and enjoying it. The focal point of such a life might be called integration, for all parts of it have fit together, one way or another. It includes the satisfaction of knowing who we are, because we know what we can do.

This life-style also includes the challenges we have met, the frustrations we have had to accept. It includes a clear sense of achievement, because we have taken advantage of the opportunities to do things that were different, interesting, and adventurous. We know what we can do and we have done most of it. If there is anything we have missed, it is not important enough for us to have seen it.

And finally, there is a traditional Vermont story of a stranger who asked an elderly Vermonter if he has always lived around here. "Well," replied the Vermonter, "not yet."

We understand what he was saying.